Dear Catherine,

"Bon Voyage" Love,

mom

Easy and Essential Greek Phrases for Beginners

Adam M. Evans

Funny helpful tips:

Practice gratitude; it's a magnet for miracles and positivity.

Understand and respect each other's values; they guide actions and decisions.

Easy and Essential Greek Phrases for Beginners : The Ultimate Guide to Mastering Conversational Greek Easily with Essential Phrases for Beginners

Life advices:

In the universe of possibilities, dream big, act with intention, and cherish the journey.

Cultivate a sense of wonder; it keeps the spirit young and vibrant.

Introduction

Καλώς ήρθατε! (Welcome!) Embrace the allure of Greece with this book, your gateway to the vibrant world of the Hellenic peninsula. Whether you are a first-time traveler or eager to deepen your cultural experience, this comprehensive guide empowers you to navigate Greece with confidence and authenticity.

Begin your journey with greetings and conversational basics, immersing yourself in the warmth of Greek hospitality. From the moment you step foot at the airport, including security procedures, and embark on your airplane journey, you'll find this phrasebook to be your trusted companion.

As you cross immigration and customs, smoothly claim your baggage, and step into a taxi or hop on a bus or train, you'll communicate effortlessly with locals and fellow travelers alike. For those looking to explore Greece by car, our phrasebook equips you to navigate car rentals and confidently drive through the picturesque landscapes.

Take to the waters with ease, whether you embark on a boat journey or indulge in a scenic cruise. Seeking directions becomes an enjoyable quest with our phrases to guide you to hidden treasures and stunning landmarks.

As the sun sets, find yourself in a comfortable hotel or hostel, or embrace the outdoors with camping under the stars. Your dining experience will be enriched with our phrases for restaurants, while poolside or at the beach, you'll immerse yourself in the relaxed Greek atmosphere.

Venture into the heart of Greek nightlife, enjoy cinematic experiences, and explore the wealth of Greek history and art in museums. Whether attending sporting events or sightseeing, express your enthusiasm in the local language.

Should you need to conduct business, go shopping, or navigate local supermarkets, our phrasebook ensures you engage with locals effectively. In times of medical needs, emergencies, or seeking assistance from the police or pharmacy, clear communication becomes your ally.

Discover the depth of Greek emotions and feelings, allowing you to connect with locals and express yourself with sincerity. Handle banking transactions, send mail at the post office, and embrace modern technology with confidence.

With cardinal and ordinal numbers, time expressions, days, months, colors, and weather descriptions at your fingertips, you'll immerse yourself in the essence of Greece.

Embrace the beauty of the Greek language and connect with the rich history and culture of this magnificent land. Whether you are a beginner or a seasoned traveler, this book invites you to unlock the treasures of Greece and embark on an unforgettable odyssey. So, καλό ταξίδι (bon voyage) and καλή διασκέδαση (happy exploring)!

Contents

PART I

GREETINGS & CONVERSATIONAL BASICS

► **Click Here for the .mp3 Audio**

Good morning – Kalimera
    Καλημέρα

Good afternoon – Kalispera
    Καλησπέρα

Good evening – Kalispera
    Καλησπέρα

Goodbye – Antio
    Αντίο

See you later – Ta leme
    Τα λέμε

See you tomorrow – Ta leme avrio
Τα λέμε αύριο

Welcome – Kalos irthes
Καλώς ήρθες

Could you talk more slowly? – Tha mporouses na milisis pio arga?
Θα μπορούσες να μιλήσεις πιο αργά

Do you understand what I am saying? – Katalavenis ti sou leo?
Καταλαβαίνεις τι σου λέω

I don't understand – Den katalaveno
Δεν καταλαβαίνω

Could you repeat that? – Mporis na to epanalavis?
Μπορείς να το επαναλάβεις

Could you please write it down? – Mporis na to grapsis se parakalo?
Μπορείς να το γράψεις σε παρακαλώ

Could you help me please? – Tha mporouses na me voithisis parakalo?
Θα μπορούσες να με βοηθήσεις παρακαλώ

Thank you for your help – Efharisto gia ti voithia sou
Ευχαριστώ για τη βοήθειά σου

Do you speak English? – Milas Agglika?
Μιλάς Αγγλικά

I speak a little Greek – Milao liga Ellinika
   Μιλάω λίγα Ελληνικά

I am on vacation – Ime diakopes
   Είμαι διακοπές

I am on a business trip – Ime se epaggelmatiko taksidi
   Είμαι σε επαγγελματικό ταξίδι

I don't know – Den ksero
   Δεν ξέρω

How old are you? – Poso chronon ise?
   Πόσο χρονών είσαι

I am (number) years old – Ime (arithmos) xronon
   Είμαι (αριθμός) χρονών

How do you say that in Greek? – Pos to les sta Ellinika?
   Πως το λες στα Ελληνικά

How are you? – Pos ise?
   Πως είσαι

Very good, thank you – Poli kala, efharisto.
   Πολύ καλά, ευχαριστώ

You're welcome – Parakalo
   Παρακαλώ

Have a nice day – Kali sou mera
    Καλή σου μέρα

What is your name? – Pio ine to onoma sou? – Pos se lene?
    Ποιο είναι το όνομα σου; - Πως σε λένε

My name is (name) – To onoma mou ine (onoma) / Me lene (onoma)
    Το όνομα μου είναι (όνομα) / Με λένε (όνομα)

Where is (place)? – Pou ine o /i / to (meros)?
    Που είναι η / ο / το (μέρος); (Note: We use different articles depending on the name of the place – feminine "i", masculine "o", "to" neuter)

I would like to introduce you to (name) – Tha ithela na se sistiso ston / stin (onoma)
    Θα ήθελα να σε συστήσω στον / στην (όνομα) (Note: The word "ston" refers to men whereas the word "stin" refers to women.)

Nice to meet you – Charika gia ti gnorimia
    Χάρηκα για τη γνωριμία

Excuse me – Me sighoris – Signomi
    Με συγχωρείς – Συγγνώμη

I am sorry – Lipamai / Signomi
    Λυπάμαι / Συγγνώμη

No problem – Kanena provlima
    Κανένα πρόβλημα

What is that? – Ti ine ekino?
  Τι είναι εκείνο

What time is it? – Ti ora ine?
  Τι ώρα είναι

Want to go eat? – Thelis na pame na fame?
  Θέλεις να πάμε να φάμε

I like that – Afto mou aresi
  Αυτό μου αρέσει

I don't like that – Den mou aresi afto
  Δεν μου αρέσει αυτό

I need information – Chriazome plirofories
  Χρειάζομαι πληροφορίες

Do you know where the (place) is? – Kseris pou ine o / i / to (meros)?
  Ξέρεις που είναι ο / η / το (μέρος); (Note: same as above about places)

What are you doing? – Ti kanis?
  Τι κάνεις

What are you going to do today? – Ti tha kanis simera?
  Τι θα κάνεις σήμερα

What do you want to do? – Ti thelis na kanis?

Τι θέλεις να κάνεις

Where are you going? – Pou pigenis?
Που πηγαίνεις

How was your day? – Pos itan i mera sou?
Πως ήταν η μέρα σου

I think so – Etsi nomizo
Έτσι νομίζω

I don't think so – De nomizo
Δε νομίζω

I need help – Thelo voithia
Θέλω βοήθεια

Where are you from? – Apo pou ise?
Από πού είσαι

I am from (place) – Ime apo ton / tin / to (meros)
Είμαι από τον / την / το (μέρος)

Do you live here? – Edo menis?
Εδώ μένεις / μένετε

Do you know this region? – Kseris afti tin periochi?
Ξέρεις αυτή την περιοχή

How long are you going to stay here? – Poso kero tha minis edo?
  Πόσο καιρό θα μείνεις εδώ

I am staying here for (number) days – Tha mino edo gia (arithmos) meres
  Θα μείνω εδώ για (αριθμός) μέρες

Do you like it around here? – Sou aresi edo?
  Σου αρέσει εδώ

Are you married or single? – Ise pantremenos i anipantros?
  Είσαι παντρεμένος ή ανύπαντρος

I am (marital status) – Ime (ikogeniaki katastasi)
  Είμαι (οικογενειακή κατάσταση)

Are you travelling by yourself? – Taksidevis monos sou?
  Ταξιδεύεις μόνος σου

Do you live with your family? – Menis me tin ikogenia sou?
  Μένεις με την οικογένεια σου

Where are you staying? – Pou menis?
  Που μένεις

What do you plan on doing while you are here? – Ti skopevis na kanis oso tha ise edo?
  Τι σκοπεύεις να κάνεις όσο θα είσαι εδώ

I am staying at (place) – Meno sto / sti (meros)

Μένω στο / στη (μέρος)

Let's keep in touch – As mi chathoume
    Ας μη χαθούμε

What is your e-mail? – Pio ine to email sou?
    Ποιο είναι το email σου

My e-mail is (email) – To email mou ine (email)
    Το email μου είναι (email)

I will write you when I get back to (place) – Tha sou grapso otan epistrepso sto / sti (meros)
    Θα σου γράψω όταν επιστρέψω στο / στη (μέρος)

What is your phone number? – Poio ine to tilefono sou?
    Ποιο είναι το τηλέφωνο σου

My phone number is (number) – To tilefono mou ine (arithmos)
    Το τηλέφωνο μου είναι (αριθμός)

Thank you for everything – Efharisto gia ola
    Ευχαριστώ για όλα

Have a good trip – Kalo taksidi
    Καλό ταξίδι

Enjoy your meal – Kali oreksi
    Καλή όρεξη

Cheers – Stin igia sou
Στην υγειά σου

Take care – Na prosehis
Να προσέχεις

Congratulations – Sigharitiria
Συγχαρητήρια

Sorry to interrupt – Signomi pou diakopto
Συγγνώμη που διακόπτω

Don't worry – Min anisihis
Μην ανησυχείς

I think so – Etsi nomizo
Έτσι νομίζω

Yes – Ne
Ναι

No – Ochi
Όχι

Maybe – Isos
Ίσως

Always – Panta
Πάντα

Never – Pote
Ποτέ

PART II

AIRPORT (INCLUDING AIRPORT SECURITY)

► **Click Here for the .mp3 Audio**

Where are the arrivals? – Pou ine i afiksis?
Που είναι οι αφίξεις

Where are the departures? – Pou ine i anahorisis?
Που είναι οι αναχωρήσεις

Where is the check-in? – Pou kanoume check-in?
Που κάνουμε check-in

Where is the information center? – Pou ine to kioski gia tis plirofories?
Που είναι το κιόσκι για τις πληροφορίες

I would like to reserve (number) tickets to (place) – Tha ithela na kliso (arithmos) isitiria gia (meros)
Θα ήθελα να κλείσω (αριθμός) εισιτήρια για (μέρος)

What is the check-in time? – Ti ora prepi na kanoume check-in?
Τι ώρα πρέπει να κάνουμε check-in

Welcome, may I have your tickets? – Kalos irthate, mporo na eho ta isitiria sas?
Καλώς ήρθατε, μπορώ να έχω τα εισιτήρια σας

I would like to buy (number) tickets to (place) – Tha ithela na agoraso (arithmos) isitiria gia (meros)
Θα ήθελα να αγοράσω (αριθμός) εισιτήρια για (μέρος)

I prefer an aisle seat – Protimo mia thesi sto diadromo
Προτιμώ μια θέση στο διάδρομο

I prefer a window seat – Protimo mia thesi sto parathiro
Προτιμώ μια θέση στο παράθυρο

How many bags do you have? – Poses tsantes ehete?
Πόσες τσάντες έχετε

I have (number) bags – Eho (aritmos) tsantes
Έχω (αριθμός) τσάντες

Can I take this as carry-on luggage? – Na to paro san chiraposkevi?
Να το πάρω σαν χειραποσκευή

I lost my boarding pass – Ehasa to isitirio mou
Έχασα το εισιτήριο μου

I missed my flight – Ehasa tin ptisi mou
Έχασα την πτήση μου

What is your destination? – Pios ine o proorismos sas?
Ποιος είναι ο προορισμός σας

This terminal is for international flights – Afti i pili ine gia diethnis ptisis
Αυτή η πύλη είναι για διεθνείς πτήσεις

This terminal is for national flights – Afti i pili ine gia ptisis entos tis horas
Αυτή η πύλη είναι για πτήσεις εντός της χώρας

Where are the luggage carts? – Pou ine ta karotsia gia tis aposkeves?
Που είναι τα καρότσια για τις αποσκευές

Can I see your passports please? – Boro na do ta diavatiria sas parakalo?
Μπορώ να δω τα διαβατήρια σας παρακαλώ

Did you have your luggage with you at all times? – Ichate tis aposkeves sinehia mazi sas?
Είχατε τις αποσκευές συνέχεια μαζί σας

How do I get to gate (Letter/Number)? – Pos boro na pao stin pili (Gramma/Arithmos)
    Πως μπορώ να πάω στην πύλη (Γράμμα/Αριθμός)

Are you carrying any weapons or firearms? – Ehete mazi sas opla?
    Έχετε μαζί σας όπλα

Are you carrying any flammable material? – Ehete mazi sas eflekta ilika?
    Έχετε μαζί σας εύφλεκτα υλικά

Are you carrying any perishable food items? – Ehete mazi sas analosima fagita?
    Έχετε μαζί σας αναλώσιμα φαγητά

Are you carrying any liquids? – Ehete mazi sas igra?
    Έχετε μαζί σας υγρά

Please take your laptop out of its case – Sas parakalo vgalte to laptop apo ti thiki tou.
    Σας παρακαλώ βγάλτε το laptop από τη θήκη του

Can you place your baggage right here? – Borite na valete tis aposkeves sas edo?
    Μπορείτε να βάλετε τις αποσκευές σας εδώ

What time do I start boarding? – Ti ora arhizei i epivivasi?
    Τι ώρα αρχίζει η επιβίβαση

Flight (number) has been delayed – I ptisi (arithmos) ehi kathisterisi

Η πτήση (αριθμός) έχει καθυστέρηση

Flight (number) has been cancelled – I ptisi (arithmos) ehi mateothi
Η πτήση (αριθμός) έχει ματαιωθεί

I had to cancel the flight because of an emergency – Eprepe na akiroso tin ptisi gia logous ektaktis anagkis
Έπρεπε να ακυρώσω την πτήση για λόγους έκτακτης ανάγκης

PART III

ON THE AIRPLANE

► **Click Here for the .mp3 Audio**

Where is seat (number)? – Pou ine i thesi (arithmos)?
    Που είναι η θέση (αριθμός)

Where is the bathroom? – Pou ine i toualetes?
    Που είναι οι τουαλέτες

Could you please fill this out? – Borite sas parakalo na to simplirosete?
    Μπορείτε σας παρακαλώ να το συμπληρώσετε

What is this form? – Ti ine afti i forma?
    Τι είναι αυτή η φόρμα

Can I have something to drink? – Boro na pio kati;

Μπορώ να πιω κάτι

Can I have something to eat? – Boro na fao kati?
   Μπορώ να φάω κάτι

What do you have to eat or drink? – Ti ehete na fame i na pioume?
   Τι έχετε να φάμε ή να πιούμε

How long until we arrive at the destination? – Poso theloume akoma na ftasoume ston proorismo mas?
   Πόσο θέλουμε ακόμα να φτάσουμε στον προορισμό μας

Could you please put that in the overhead locker? – Borite sas parakalo na to valete sto ntoulapi gia tis chiraposkeves?
   Μπορείτε σας παρακαλώ να το βάλετε στο ντουλάπι για τις χειραποσκευές

The captain has turned on/off the fasten seatbelt sign – O kivernitis echi anapsi tin endiksi gia ti zoni
   Ο κυβερνήτης έχει ανάψει την ένδειξη για τη ζώνη

Please turn off all electronic devices – Parakalo kliste oles tis ilektronikes siskeves
   Παρακαλώ κλείστε όλες τις ηλεκτρονικές συσκευές

We are experiencing some turbulence – Echoume liges anataraksis
   Έχουμε λίγες αναταράξεις

Please fasten your seatbelts – Parakalo deste ti zoni sas
   Παρακαλώ δέστε τη ζώνη σας

PART IV

IMMIGRATION & CUSTOMS

► <u>**Click Here for the .mp3 Audio**</u>

Where is immigration? – Pou ine to tmima metanastefseon?
   Που είναι το τμήμα μεταναστεύσεων

Where is customs? – Pou ine to telonio?
   Που είναι το τελωνείο

What is the purpose of your trip? – Pios ine o skopos tou taksidiou sas?
   Ποιος είναι ο σκοπός του ταξιδιού σας

I am visiting friends – Episkeftomai kapious filous
   Επισκέπτομαι κάποιους φίλους

I am on vacation – Irtha gia diakopes

Ήρθα για διακοπές

I am on a business trip – Ime se epagelmatiko taksidi
  Είμαι σε επαγγελματικό ταξίδι

What do you do for work? – Ti doulia kanis?
  Τι δουλειά κάνεις

How long will you be here? – Poso kero tha minis edo?
  Πόσο καιρό θα μείνεις εδώ

I will be staying here (number) days – Tha mino (arithmos) meres.
  Θα μείνω (αριθμός) μέρες

Have you ever been here before? – Echis ksanaerthi edo?
  Έχεις ξαναέρθει εδώ

Can you open this bag for me? – Borite na aniksete tin tsanta gia emena?
  Μπορείτε να ανοίξετε την τσάντα για εμένα

Are you traveling alone? – Taksidevete monos/moni? (Note: "monos" refers to men, "moni" refers to women)
  Ταξιδεύετε μόνος / μόνη

I am traveling with (names) – Taksidevo me ton / tin / tous (onomata) (Note: "ton" refers to a man's name, "tin" refers to a woman's name, "tous" refers to many people)
  Ταξιδεύω με τον / την / τους (ονόματα)

I need an interpreter – Chriazome enan dierminea
   Χρειάζομαι έναν διερμηνέα

Do you have anything to declare? – Echete na dilosete kati?
   Έχετε να δηλώσετε κάτι

Did you fill out the customs form? – Simplirosate tin etisi tou teloniou?
   Συμπληρώσατε την αίτηση του τελωνείου

PART V

BAGGAGE CLAIM

► **Click Here for the .mp3 Audio**

Where can I claim my baggage? – Apo pou boro na paro tis aposkeves mou?
  Από πού μπορώ να πάρω τις αποσκευές μου

Is that your baggage? – Ekines ine i aposkeves sas?
  Εκείνες είναι οι αποσκευές σας

These are my suitcases – Aftes ine i valitses mou
  Αυτές είναι οι βαλίτσες μου

Do you need help with your luggage? – Chriazeste voithia me tis aposkeves sas?
  Χρειάζεστε βοήθεια με τις αποσκευές σας

Could you please help me with my luggage? – Tha borousate na me voithisete me tis aposkeves mou?
Θα μπορούσατε να με βοηθήσετε με τις αποσκευές μου

How much luggage do you have? – Poses aposkeves echete?
Πόσες αποσκευές έχετε

Where are the luggage carts? – Pou ine ta karotsia gia tis aposkeves?
Που είναι τα καρότσια για τις αποσκευές

Do you have your baggage ticket? – Echeis to aftokolito ton aposkevon?
Έχεις το αυτοκόλλητο των αποσκευών

Where is my luggage? – Pou ine i aposkeves mou?
Που είναι οι αποσκευές μου

My luggage hasn't arrived – I aposkeves mou den ehoun ftasi
Οι αποσκευές μου δεν έχουν φτάσει

My luggage has been damaged – I aposkeves mou ehoun iposti zimia
Οι αποσκευές μου έχουν υποστεί ζημιά

PART VI

TAXI

► **Click Here for the .mp3 Audio**

Where can I get a taxi? – Pou boro na vro taxi?
   Που μπορώ να βρω ταξί

Can you call me a taxi? – Boris na mou kalesis ena taxi?
   Μπορείς να μου καλέσεις ένα ταξί

Do you know where I can call to order a taxi? – Kseris pou boro na kaleso gia taxi?
   Ξέρεις που μπορώ να καλέσω για ταξί

Where are you going to? – Pou pigenis?
   Που πηγαίνεις

Do you have a meter? – Echis taximetro?

Έχεις ταξίμετρο

Do you use the meter? – Chrisimopiis taximetro?
   Χρησιμοποιείς ταξίμετρο

Can you take me to the airport? – Boris na me pas sto aerodromio?
   Μπορείς να με πας στο αεροδρόμιο

Can you take me downtown? – Boris na me pas sto kentro?
   Μπορείς να με πας στο κέντρο

Can you take me to the hospital? – Boris na me pas sto nosokomio?
   Μπορείς να με πας στο νοσοκομείο

Can you take me to the shopping mall? – Boris na me pas sto eboriko kentro?
   Μπορείς να με πας στο εμπορικό κέντρο

Can you take me to the police station? – Boris na me pas sto astinomiko tmima?
   Μπορείς να με πας στο αστυνομικό τμήμα

Can you take me to the bank? – Boris na me pas stin trapeza?
   Μπορείς να με πας στην τράπεζα

Can you take me to the post office? – Boris na me pas sto tachidromio?
   Μπορείς να με πας στο ταχυδρομείο

Can you take me to the museum? – Boris na me pas sto mousio?

Μπορείς να με πας στο μουσείο

Can you take me to the aquarium? – Boris na me pas sto enidrio?
Μπορείς να με πας στο ενυδρείο

Can you take me to (place)? – Boris na me pas sto / sti (meros)?
Μπορείς να με πας στο / στη (μέρος)

How much does it cost to go to (place)? – Poso kostizi mehri to / ti (meros)?
Πόσο κοστίζει μέχρι το / τη (μέρος)

Do you have change for a (number) bill? – Echis psila gia ena (arithmos) chartonomisma?
Έχεις ψιλά για ένα (αριθμός) χαρτονόμισμα

Can you please write down the total? – Boris se parakalo na simiosis to sinolo?
Μπορείς σε παρακαλώ να σημειώσεις το σύνολο

Can you take the quickest route? – Boris na pas apo ton pio sintomo dromo?
Μπορείς να πας από τον πιο σύντομο δρόμο

Can we drive past (place) on the way? – Boroume na perasoume apo to / ti (meros) kathos pigenoume eki?
Μπορούμε να περάσουμε από το / τη (μέρος) καθώς πηγαίνουμε εκεί

I am in a hurry – Viazome

Βιάζομαι

Could you stop here? – Tha mporouses na stamatisis edo?
   Θα μπορούσες να σταματήσεις εδώ

Stop at the next traffic light – Stamata sto epomeno fanari
   Σταμάτα στο επόμενο φανάρι

Can you please wait? – Boris na perimenis se parakalo?
   Μπορείς να περιμένεις σε παρακαλώ

Keep the change – Krata ta resta
   Κράτα τα ρέστα

Here's a tip – Oriste ena filodorima
   Ορίστε ένα φιλοδώρημα

Can you pick me up in (number) minutes? – Boris na erthis na me paris se (arithmos) lepta?
   Μπορείς να έρθεις να με πάρεις σε (αριθμός) λεπτά

Can you drive slower? – Boris na pas pio arga?
   Μπορείς να πας πιο αργά

Can you drive faster? – Boris na pas pio grigora?
   Μπορείς να πας πιο γρήγορα

PART VII

BUS

► **Click Here for the .mp3 Audio**

Where is the bus terminal? – Pou ine o stathmos ton leoforion?
   Που είναι ο σταθμός των λεωφορείων

Where can I buy a ticket? – Apo pou boro na agoraso eisitirio?
   Από πού μπορώ να αγοράσω εισιτήριο

Where is the bus stop? – Pou ine i stasi gia to leoforio?
   Που είναι η στάση για το λεωφορείο

Which bus passes through here? – Pio leoforio pernai apo eki?
   Ποιο λεωφορείο περνάει από εκεί

Can I get a ticket to (place)? – Boro na echo ena isitirio gia (meros)?
   Μπορώ να έχω ένα εισιτήριο για (μέρος)

27

I would like to change my ticket – Tha ithela na alakso to isitirio mou
Θα ήθελα να αλλάξω το εισιτήριο μου

I would like to cancel my ticket – Tha ithela na akiroso to isitirio mou
Θα ήθελα να ακυρώσω το εισιτήριο μου

Is it a direct route? – Ine apefthias diadromi?
Είναι απευθείας διαδρομή

Do I have to change buses? – Prepi na alakso leoforio?
Πρέπει να αλλάξω λεωφορείο

Where does this bus go to? – Pou pigeni afto to leoforio?
Που πηγαίνει αυτό το λεωφορείο

Which bus goes to (place)? – Pio leoforio pigeni sto / sti (meros)?
Ποιο λεωφορείο πηγαίνει στο / στη (μέρος)

Does this bus stop in (place)? – Stamatai to leoforio sto / sti (meros)?
Σταματάει το λεωφορείο στο / στη (μέρος)

What time does it get to (place)? – Ti ora ftani sto / sti (meros)?
Τι ώρα φτάνει στο / στη (μέρος)

Where does the bus to (place) leave from? – Apo pou fevgi to leoforio gia (meros)?
Από πού φεύγει το λεωφορείο για (μέρος)

At what time does the bus to (place) leave? – Ti ora fevgi to leoforio gia (meros)?

 Τι ώρα φεύγει το λεωφορείο για (μέρος)

Why is the bus taking so long? – Giati argi to leoforio?

 Γιατί αργεί το λεωφορείο

How long is the ride? – Poso diarki i diadromi?

 Πόσο διαρκεί η διαδρομή

Is this seat available? – I thesi ine piasmeni?

 Η θέση είναι πιασμένη

Can I get an aisle seat? – Boro na echo mia thesi ston diadromo?

 Μπορώ να έχω μια θέση στον διάδρομο

Can I get a window seat? - Boro na echo mia thesi sto parathiro?

 Μπορώ να έχω μια θέση στο παράθυρο

How much does the bus fare cost? – Poso kani to isitirio gia ta leoforia?

 Πόσο κάνει το εισιτήριο για τα λεωφορεία

Can you tell me when we get to (place)? – Boris na mou pis otan ftasoume sto / sti (meros)?

 Μπορείς να μου πεις όταν φτάσουμε στο/στη (μέρος)

This is my stop – Afti ine i stasi mou

 Αυτή είναι η στάση μου

Can I get off here? – Boro na katevo edo?
Μπορώ να κατέβω εδώ

Could you please stop here? – Boris na stamatisis edo se parakalo?
Μπορείς να σταματήσεις εδώ σε παρακαλώ

Can you turn on the air conditioning? – Boris na anapsis to klimatistiko?
Μπορείς να ανάψεις το κλιματιστικό

Can you turn off the air conditioning? - Boris na klisis to klimatistiko?
Μπορείς να κλείσεις το κλιματιστικό

PART VIII

TRAIN

► **Click Here for the .mp3 Audio**

Where is the train station? – Pou ine o stathmos ton trenon?
  Που είναι ο σταθμός των τρένων

Which train goes to (place)? – Pio treno pigeni sto / sti (meros)?
  Ποιο τρένο πηγαίνει στο / στη (μέρος)

Where can I buy a ticket? – Apo pou boro na agoraso isitirio?
  Από πού μπορώ να αγοράσω εισιτήριο

I would like to change my ticket – Tha ithela na alakso to isitirio mou.
  Θα ήθελα να αλλάξω το εισιτήριο μου

I would like to cancel my ticket – Tha ithela na akiroso to isitirio mou.
  Θα ήθελα να ακυρώσω το εισιτήριο μου

Where does the train to (place) leave from? – Apo pou fevgi to treno gia (meros)?
    Από πού φεύγει το τρένο για (μέρος)

At what time does the train to (place) leave? – Ti ora fevgi to treno gia (meros)?
    Τι ώρα φεύγει το τρένο για (μέρος)

How much does the train fare cost? – Poso kostizi ena isitirio gia to treno?
    Πόσο κοστίζει ένα εισιτήριο για το τρένο

When does the train pass? – Pote pernai to treno?
    Πότε περνάει το τρένο

How long does the train take to get to (place)? – Posi ora kani to treno gia na ftasi sto / sti (meros)?
    Πόση ώρα κάνει το τρένο για να φτάσει στο / στη (μέρος)

This is the last stop – Afti ine I teleftea stasi
    Αυτή είναι η τελευταία στάση

Is this seat available? – Ine piasmeni i thesi?
    Είναι πιασμένη η θέση

PART IX

CAR RENTAL

► **Click Here for the .mp3 Audio**

Where can I rent a car? – Pou boro na nikiaso ena amaxi?
   Που μπορώ να νοικιάσω ένα αμάξι

What time does the car rental place open? – Ti ora anigi to grafio enikiasis aftokiniton?
   Τι ώρα ανοίγει το γραφείο ενοικίασης αυτοκινήτων

What time does the car rental place close? - Ti ora klini to grafio enikiasis aftokiniton?
   Τι ώρα κλείνει το γραφείο ενοικίασης αυτοκινήτων

I would like to rent a car – Tha ithela na nikiaso ena aftokinito
   Θα ήθελα να νοικιάσω ένα αυτοκίνητο

I would like to rent a motorbike – Tha ithela na nikiaso ena michanaki
  Θα ήθελα να νοικιάσω ένα μηχανάκι

I would like to rent an automatic car – Tha ithela na nikiaso ena aftomato aftokinito
  Θα ήθελα να νοικιάσω ένα αυτόματο αυτοκίνητο

I would like to rent a manual car – Tha ithela na nikiaso ena aftokinito me tachitites
  Θα ήθελα να νοικιάσω ένα αυτοκίνητο με ταχύτητες

Which car would you recommend? – Pio amaxi protinis?
  Ποιο αμάξι προτείνεις

What year is it from? – Pias chronias ine?
  Ποιας χρονιάς είναι

What model is it? – Ti modelo ine?
  Τι μοντέλο είναι

Do you have a car with air conditioner? – Echete amaxi me air condition (klimatismo)?
  Έχετε αμάξι με air condition (κλιματισμό)

What do I need to rent a car? – Ti chriazete gia na nikiaso ena aftokinito?
  Τι χρειάζεται για να νοικιάσω ένα αυτοκίνητο

How much does it cost to rent the car for a day? – Poso kostizi gia na nikiaso to amaxi gia mia mera?
Πόσο κοστίζει για να νοικιάσω το αμάξι για μία μέρα

How much does it cost to rent the car for a week? - Poso kostizi gia na nikiaso to amaxi mia evdomada?
Πόσο κοστίζει να νοικιάσω το αμάξι μία εβδομάδα

How much does it cost to rent the car for a month? - Poso kostizi gia na nikiaso to amaxi gia ena mina?
Πόσο κοστίζει για να νοικιάσω το αμάξι για ένα μήνα

Is the insurance included in the price? – I asfalia perilamvanete stin timi?
Η ασφάλεια περιλαμβάνεται στην τιμή

How much does the insurance cost? – Poso kostizi i asfalia?
Πόσο κοστίζει η ασφάλεια

I need to rent the car for (number) days – Chriazomai to amaxi gia (arithmos) meres.
Χρειάζομαι το αμάξι για (αριθμός) μέρες

Please show me your passport – Dikse mou to diavatirio sou se parakalo.
Δείξε μου το διαβατήριο σου σε παρακαλώ

Do you take credit cards? – Decheste pistotikes kartes?
Δέχεστε πιστωτικές κάρτες

Is the tank full? – Ine gemato?
  Είναι γεματό

Please reserve a car for me – Kratise ena amaksi gia emena parakalo
  Κράτησε ένα αμάξι για εμένα παρακαλώ

Can I drop the car off at the airport? – Boro na afiso to amaksi sto aerodromio?
  Μπορώ να αφήσω το αμάξι στο αεροδρόμιο

PART X

CARS & DRIVING

► **Click Here for the .mp3 Audio**

Is there a service station nearby? – Iparhi edo konta venzinadiko?
    Υπάρχει εδώ κοντά βενζινάδικο

I need gasoline – Chriazome venzini
    Χρειάζομαι βενζίνη

I need diesel – Chriazome petreleo
    Χρειάζομαι πετρέλαιο

I need unleaded gas – Chriazome amolivdi
    Χρειάζομαι αμόλυβδη

Can you give me (money) worth of gasoline? – Boris na mou valis venzini gia (lefta)?

Μπορείς να μου βάλεις βενζίνη για (λεφτά)

Can you give me (number) gallons of gasoline? – Boris na mou dosis (arithmos) litra venzini?
Μπορείς να μου δώσεις (αριθμός) λίτρα βενζίνη

Can you fill it up? – Boris na to gemisis?
Μπορείς να το γεμίσεις

Can you check my car levels? – Boris na elegxis ta ladia tou aftokinitou?
Μπορείς να ελέγξεις τα λάδια του αυτοκινήτου

Where can I check my tire pressure? – Boris na elegxis ton aera sta lastiha?
Μπορείς να ελέγξεις τον αέρα στα λάστιχα

Where can I put air to my tires? – Pou boro na fouskoso ta lastiha?
Που μπορώ να φουσκώσω τα λάστιχα

Where do I pay? – Pou plirono?
Που πληρώνω

I ran out of gas – Emina apo venzini
Έμεινα από βενζίνη

I am in a traffic jam – Echi kinisi
Έχει κίνηση

How do I get to (place)? – Pos tha pao sto / sti (meros)?

Πως θα πάω στο / στη (μέρος)

Is this the road to (place)? – Aftos ine o dromos gia (meros)?
　　Αυτός είναι ο δρόμος για (μέρος)

The road is closed – O dromos ine klistos
　　Ο δρόμος είναι κλειστός

Where can I get a road map? – Pou boro na vro ena charti?
　　Που μπορώ να βρω ένα χάρτη

What is the speed limit here? – Pio ine to orio tachititas edo?
　　Ποιο είναι το όριο ταχύτητας εδώ

Is there a parking lot near here? – Iparhi parking edo konta?
　　Υπάρχει παρκινγκ εδώ κοντά

Is the parking lot open all night? – To parking ine anihto olo to vradi?
　　Το παρκινγκ είναι ανοιχτό όλο το βράδυ

Can I park here? – Boro na parkaro edo?
　　Μπορώ να παρκάρω εδώ

How long can I park here? – Posi ora boro na parkaro edo?
　　Πόση ώρα μπορώ να παρκάρω εδώ

Can I leave my car here? – Boro na afiso to amaxi mou edo?
　　Μπορώ να αφήσω το αμάξι μου εδώ

We had an accident – Ichame ena atichima
Είχαμε ένα ατύχημα

Nobody is hurt – De chtipise kanenas
Δε χτύπησε κανένας

Is your car insured? – To amaxi sou echi asfalia?
Το αμάξι σου έχει ασφάλεια

Here are my insurance details – Edo ine ta stichia tis asfalias mou
Εδώ είναι τα στοιχεία της ασφάλειας μου

My car broke down – Chalase to amaxi mou
Χάλασε το αμάξι μου

My car doesn't star – To amaxi mou den perni brosta
Το αμάξι μου δεν παίρνει μπροστά

My car overheated – To amaxi mou zestathike
Το αμάξι μου ζεστάθηκε

My car won't brake – De litourgoun ta frena tou aftokinitou
Δεν λειτουργούν τα φρένα του αυτοκινήτου

My car's fan belts broke – Kopike o imantas tou aftokinitou
Κόπηκε ο ιμάντας του αυτοκινήτου

My car's gear shift is stuck – Kolise o levies tachititon
Κόλλησε ο λεβιές ταχυτήτων

My car's clutch isn't working – De litourgi o simplektis
Δε λειτουργεί ο συμπλέκτης

The car is letting out a lot of smoke – To amaxi vgazi kapnous
Το αμάξι βγάζει καπνούς

I left the keys locked inside – Afisa ta klidia mesa sto amaxi. /
Klidothika apexo.
Άφησα τα κλειδιά μέσα στο αμάξι./Κλειδώθηκα απ'έξω

My car battery is dead – Emina apo bataria.
Έμεινα από μπαταρία

I have a flat tire – Epatha lasticho.
Έπαθα λάστιχο

I need a jack – Chriazome ena grilo.
Χρειάζομαι έναν γρύλο

I don't have a spare tire – Den echo rezerva
Δεν έχω ρεζέρβα

My windshield wipers don't work – De litourgoun i gialokatharistires
Δε λειτουργούν οι γυαλοκαθαριστήρες

I need a tow car – Chriazome ena gerano
Χρειάζομαι ένα γερανό

I need a mechanic – Chriazome enan michaniko
Χρειάζομαι έναν μηχανικό

Is there a mechanic nearby? – Iparchi michanikos edo konta?
  Υπάρχει μηχανικός εδώ κοντά

Do you know what is wrong with it? – Xeris ti provlima echi?
  Ξέρεις τι πρόβλημα έχει

Can you fix it? – Boris na to ftiaxis?
  Μπορείς να το φτιάξεις

Where can I get this fixed? – Pou boro na to episkevaso?
  Που μπορώ να το επισκευάσω

Can I still drive it? – Boro akomi na to odigiso?
  Μπορώ ακόμη να το οδηγήσω

How long will it take to fix? – Poso tha chriastis na to episkevasis?
  Πόσο θα χρειαστείς να το επισκευάσεις

Can you repair it today? – Boris na to ftiaxis simera?
  Μπορείς να το φτιάξεις σήμερα

When can I pick it up? – Pote boro na to paro?
  Πότε μπορώ να το πάρω

How much will the fix cost? – Poso tha kostisi i episkevi?
  Πόσο θα κοστίσει η επισκευή

How much does this spare part cost? – Poso kani to antalaktiko?
  Πόσο κάνει το ανταλλακτικό

Where can I buy the spare part? – Apo pou boro na agoraso to antalaktiko?

Από πού μπορώ να αγοράσω το ανταλλακτικό

PART XI

BOATS & CRUISES

► **Click Here for the .mp3 Audio**

Where is the harbor? – Pou ine to limani?
    Που είναι το λιμάνι

Where do I buy tickets for a cruise? – Apo pou tha agoraso isitiria gia mia krouaziera?
    Από πού θα αγοράσω εισιτήρια για μια κρουαζιέρα

Where do I buy tickets for a boat ride? – Apo pou tha agoraso isitiria gia mia volta me to plio?
    Από πού θα αγοράσω εισιτήρια για μια βόλτα με το πλοίο

Where do the boats go to? – Pou pigenoun ta plia?
    Που πηγαίνουν τα πλοία

How much does a ticket cost? – Poso kostizi ena isitirio?
   Πόσο κοστίζει ένα εισιτήριο

Can I have (number) tickets for the boat to (place)? – Boro na echo (arithmos) isitiria gia to plio pros (meros)?
   Μπορώ να έχω (αριθμός) εισιτήρια για το πλοίο προς (μέρος)

Can I have (number) tickets for the cruise? – Boro na echo (arithmos) isitiria gia tin krouaziera?
   Μπορώ να έχω (αριθμός) εισιτήρια για την κρουαζιέρα

Will I need my passport? – Tha chriasto diavatirio?
   Θα χρειαστώ διαβατήριο

When will the boat leave? – Pote tha figi to plio?
   Πότε θα φύγει το πλοίο

When will the cruise leave? – Pote tha figi to krouazieroplio?
   Πότε θα φύγει το κρουαζιερόπλοιο

Where will the boat leave from? – Apo pou tha figi to plio?
   Από πού θα φύγει το πλοίο

Where will the cruise leave from? – Apo pou tha figi to krouazieroplio?
   Από πού θα φύγει το κρουαζιερόπλοιο

How long is the boat ride? – Poso diarki to taksidi me to plio?
   Πόσο διαρκεί το ταξίδι με το πλοίο

How long is the cruise? – Poso diarki i krouaziera?
   Πόσο διαρκεί η κρουαζιέρα

What does the cruise come with? – Ti perilamvani i krouaziera?
   Τι περιλαμβάνει η κρουαζιέρα

What can the kids do in the cruise? – Ti boroun na kanoun ta pedia stin krouaziera?
   Τι μπορούν να κάνουν τα παιδιά στην κρουαζιέρα

Does the cruise come with the drinks? – I krouaziera perilamvani kai pota?
   Η κρουαζιέρα περιλαμβάνει και ποτά

Does the cruise come with the food? - I krouaziera perilamvani kai fagito?
   Η κρουαζιέρα περιλαμβάνει και φαγητό

How much does the food cost? – Poso kostizi to fagito?
   Πόσο κοστίζει το φαγητό

How much do the drinks cost? – Poso kostizoun ta pota?
   Πόσο κοστίζουν τα ποτά

Will there be Internet access on the cruise? – Tha iparchi internet sto plio?
   Θα υπάρχει ίντερνετ στο πλοίο

Will there be television on board? – Tha iparchi tileorasi sto plio?
   Θα υπάρχει τηλεόραση στο πλοίο

Will there be gambling on the cruise? – Tha iparchi kazino sto plio?
Θα υπάρχει καζίνο στο πλοίο

Are there any restrictions on how much luggage I can take? – Iparchi periorismos ston arithmo ton aposkevon pou boro na echo mazi mou?
Υπάρχει περιορισμός στον αριθμό των αποσκευών που μπορώ να έχω μαζί μου

Are there any restrictions on what I can take? – Iparchoun periorismi shetika me ta pragmata pou boro na paro mazi mou?
Υπάρχουν περιορισμοί σχετικά με τα πράγματα που μπορώ να πάρω μαζί μου

Where are the life vests? – Pou ine ta sosivia?
Που είναι τα σωσίβια

What should we do in case of an emergency? – Ti prepi na kanoume se periptosi ektaktis anagkis?
Τι πρέπει να κάνουμε σε περίπτωση έκτακτης ανάγκης

What can I do to prevent getting seasick? – Ti boro na kano gia na mi me piasi naftia?
Τι μπορώ να κάνω για να μη με πιάσει ναυτία;

I feel seasick – Me pirakse i thalassa. / Echo naftia.
Με πείραξε η θάλασσα. / Έχω ναυτία

Is the cruise safe? – I krouaziera ine asfalis?
Η κρουαζιέρα είναι ασφαλής

What will we see along the way? – Ti tha doume sto taxidi?
   Τι θα δούμε στο ταξίδι

PART XII

ASKING DIRECTIONS

► <u>**Click Here for the .mp3 Audio**</u>

Where is this address? – Pou vriskete afti I diefthinsi?
   Που βρίσκεται αυτή η διεύθυνση

How do I get to this address? – Pos boro na pao se afti ti diefthinsi?
   Πως μπορώ να πάω σε αυτή τη διεύθυνση

What is the address? – Pia ine I diefthinsi?
   Ποια είναι η διεύθυνση

How do I get to downtown? – Pos boro na pao sto kentro?
   Πως μπορώ να πάω στο κέντρο

How do I get to (place)? – Pos boro na pao sto/sti (meros)?
   Πως μπορώ να πάω στο/στη (μέρος)

Where can I get a city map? – Pou boro na vro ena charti tis polis?
Που μπορώ να βρω ένα χάρτη της πόλης

Can you show me on the map? – Boris na mou dixis sto charti?
Μπορείς να μου δείξεις στο χάρτη

Is it far? – Ine makria?
Είναι μακριά

Where can I get a map? – Pou boro na vro ena charti?
Που μπορώ να βρω ένα χάρτη

Can I walk there? – Boro na perpatiso mechri eki?
Μπορώ να περπατήσω μέχρι εκεί

Am I going the right direction? – Pigeno pros ti sosti katefthinsi?
Πηγαίνω προς τη σωστή κατεύθυνση

Where is a restaurant? – Pou boro na vro ena estiatorio?
Που μπορώ να βρω ένα εστιατόριο

Where is a store? – Pou boro na vro ena magazi?
Που μπορώ να βρω ένα μαγαζί

Where is the police station? – Pou ine to astinomiko tmima?
Που είναι το αστυνομικό τμήμα

Where is the hospital? – Pou ine to nosokomio?
Που είναι το νοσοκομείο

Where is the pharmacy? – Pou ine to farmakio?
Που είναι το φαρμακείο

Where is a fast food place? – Pou boro na vro ena fast foodadiko?
Που μπορώ να βρω ένα φαστ-φουντάδικο

Where is a supermarket? – Pou echi supermarket?
Που έχει σούπερ μάρκετ

Where is a park? – Pou echi parko?
Που έχει πάρκο

Where is a shopping mall? – Pou ine to emporiko kentro?
Που είναι το εμπορικό κέντρο

Where is a bank? – Pou boro na vro mia trapeza?
Που μπορώ να βρω μια τράπεζα

Where is an atm? - Pou boro na vro ena ATM?
Που μπορώ να βρω ένα ATM

Where is a hotel? - Pou boro na vro ena xenodochio?
Που μπορώ να βρω ένα ξενοδοχείο

Where is a gas station? - Pou boro na vro ena venzinadiko?
Που μπορώ να βρω ένα βενζινάδικο

Where can I rent a car? – Pou boro na nikiaso ena aftokinito?
Που μπορώ να νοικιάσω ένα αυτοκίνητο

Where is a bar? - Pou boro na vro ena bar?
Που μπορώ να βρω ένα μπαρ

Where is a nightclub? - Pou boro na vro ena nightclub?
Που μπορώ να βρω ένα κλαμπ

Where is the airport? – Pou ine to aerodromio?
Που είναι το αεροδρόμιο

Where is the museum? – Pou ine to mousio?
Που είναι το μουσείο

Where is the zoo? – Pou ine o zoologikos kipos?
Που είναι ο ζωολογικός κήπος

Where is the aquarium? – Pou ine to enidrio?
Που είναι το ενυδρείο

Where is the amusement park? – Pou ine to luna park?
Που είναι το λούνα παρκ

Where is the train station? – Pou ine o stathmos ton trenon?
Που είναι ο σταθμός των τρένων

Where is the bus stop? – Pou ine i stasi tou leoforiou?
Που είναι η στάση του λεωφορείου

Where is a restroom? – Pou ine i dimosies toualetes?
Που είναι οι δημόσιες τουάλετες

Where can I rent a bicycle? – Pou boro na nikiaso ena podilato?
    Που μπορώ να νοικιάσω ένα ποδήλατο

Go straight (number) blocks – Se (aritmos) tetragona
    Σε (αριθμός) τετράγωνα

Turn to the left – Stripse aristera
    Στρίψε αριστερά

Turn to the right – Stripse dexia
    Στρίψε δεξιά

It is around the corner – Ine sti gonia
    Είναι στη γωνία

Where are we? – Pou imaste?
    Που είμαστε

I am lost – Chathika
    Χάθηκα

PART XIII

HOTEL & HOSTEL

► **Click Here for the .mp3 Audio**

Where can I find a hotel? – Pou boro na vro ena xenodochio?
   Που μπορώ να βρω ένα ξενοδοχείο

Where can I find a hostel? – Pou boro na vro enan xenona?
   Που μπορώ να βρω ένα ξενώνα

I would like to register – Tha ithela na ipograpso
   Θα ήθελα να υπογράψω

I have a reservation under the (name) – Echo kani kratisi me to onoma (onoma)
   Έχω κάνει κράτηση με το όνομα (όνομα)

What is my room number? – Pio ine to domatio mou?

Ποιο είναι το δωμάτιο μου

Do you have a room available for (number)? – Echete diathesimo domatio gia (arithmos) atoma?
Έχετε διαθέσιμο δωμάτιο για (αριθμός) άτομα

How much does it cost per night? – Poso stixizi ti vradia?
Πόσο στοιχίζει τη βραδιά

Do you have a room with an air conditioner? – Echete domatia me air condition (klimatismo)?
Έχετε δωμάτια με air condition (κλιματισμό)

Can three people stay in this room? – Boroun na minoun tria atoma se afto to domatio?
Μπορούν να μείνουν τρία άτομα σε αυτό το δωμάτιο

Could I see the room? – Tha borousa na do to domatio?
Θα μπορούσα να δω το δωμάτιο

Is the food included? – To fagito perilamvanete stin timi?
Το φαγητό περιλαμβάνεται στην τιμή

Is there a strong box in the room? – Iparchi chrimatokivotio sto domatio?
Υπάρχει χρηματοκιβώτιο στο δωμάτιο

Is there car parking available? – Iparchi parking gia ta aftokinita?
Υπάρχει πάρκινγκ για τα αυτοκίνητα

What time is the check-out? – Ti ora prepi na afiso to domatio?
   Τι ώρα πρέπει να αφήσω το δωμάτιο

Do I have to pay upfront? – Prepi na sas pliroso prokatavolika?
   Πρέπει να σας πληρώσω προκαταβολικά

When is breakfast served? – Ti ora servirete to proino?
   Τι ώρα σερβίρετε το πρωινό

I'll take it – Tha to paro
   Θα το πάρω

What does the room come with? – Ti perilamvani i timi tou domatiou?
   Τι περιλαμβάνει η τιμή του δωματίου

Do you have a gym? – Echete gimnastirio?
   Έχετε γυμναστήριο

Do you have a pool? – Echete pisina?
   Έχετε πισίνα

Do you have a laundry room? – Echete choro gia plintiria?
   Έχετε χώρο για πλυντήρια

Do you have a conference room? – Echete choro gia sinedria?
   Έχετε χώρο για συνέδρια

Can I get help with the luggage? – Boro na echo ligi voithia me tis aposkeves?

Μπορώ να έχω λίγη βοήθεια με τις αποσκευές

Single room – Monoklino
Μονόκλινο

Double room – Diklino
Δίκλινο

Full Board / Half Board – Diamoni kai gevmata / Diamoni kai proino
Διαμονή και γεύματα / Διαμονή και πρωινό

Is there room service? – Iparchi ipiresia domatiou?
Υπάρχει υπηρεσία δωματίου

Can you please send me (item/food)? – Borite na mou stilete
(pragma/fagito)?
Μπορείτε να μου στείλετε (πράγμα/φαγητό)

Could you wake me up at (time)? – Tha borousate na me ksipnisete
stis (ora)?
Θα μπορούσατε να με ξυπνήσετε στις (ώρα)

The room is too hot– Echi poli zesti sto domatio
Έχει πολύ ζέστη στο δωμάτιο

The room is too cold – Echi poli krio sto domatio
Έχει πολύ κρύο στο δωμάτιο

The room is too noisy – Echi poli fasaria sto domatio
Έχει πολύ φασαρία στο δωμάτιο

The room is too dirty – To domatio ine vromiko
   Το δωμάτιο είναι βρώμικο

The room smells very bad – To domatio mirizi aschima
   Το δωμάτιο μυρίζει άσχημα

The room is not organized – To domatio ine akatastato
   Το δωμάτιο είναι ακατάστατο

The key doesn't work – De doulevi to klidi
   Δε δουλεύει το κλειδί

I lost the key – Echasa to klidi
   Έχασα το κλειδί

The fan doesn't work – De doulevi o anemistiras
   Δε δουλεύει ο ανεμιστήρας

The TV doesn't work – De doulevi i tileorasi
   Δε δουλεύει η τηλεόραση

The phone doesn't work – De litourgi to tilefono
   Δε λειτουργεί το τηλέφωνο

The refrigerator doesn't work – To psigio de litourgi
   Το ψυγείο δε λειτουργεί

There is no hot water in the bathroom – Den iparchi zesto nero sto banio
   Δεν υπάρχει ζεστό νερό στο μπάνιο

There is no soap in the bathroom – Den iparchi sapouni sto banio
 Δεν υπάρχει σαπούνι στο μπάνιο

There is no toilet paper in the bathroom – Den iparchi charti toualetas sto banio
 Δεν υπάρχει χαρτί τουαλέτας στο μπάνιο

There are no towels in the room – Den iparchoun petsetes sto domatio
 Δεν υπάρχουν πετσέτες στο δωμάτιο

The towels smell bad – I petsetes mirizoun aschima
 Οι πετσέτες μυρίζουν άσχημα

The towels are not clean – I petsetes ine vromikes
 Οι πετσέτες είναι βρώμικες

Could you give me another blanket? – Tha borousa na echo alli mia kouverta?
 Θα μπορούσα να έχω άλλη μια κουβέρτα

Can I change rooms? – Boro na alaxo domatio?
 Μπορώ να αλλάξω δωμάτιο

Where do I pay? – Pou plirono?
 Που πληρώνω

Could you give me the bill please? – Tha borousate na mou dosete to logariasmo?
 Θα μπορούσατε να μου δώσετε το λογαριασμό

Do you take credit cards? – Decheste pistotikes kartes?
Δέχεστε πιστωτικές κάρτες

I am going to pay in cash – Tha pliroso me metrita
Θα πληρώσω με μετρητά

Could I check out later? – Tha borousa na afiso to domatio ligo argotera?
Θα μπορούσα να αφήσω το δωμάτιο λίγο αργότερα

Can I leave my luggage until (time)? - Boro na afiso tis aposkeves mou mechri tis (ora)?
Μπορώ να αφήσω τις αποσκευές μου μέχρι τις (ώρα)

May we have our passports back? – Boroume na paroume ta diavatiria mas?
Μπορούμε να πάρουμε τα διαβατήρια μας

Could you give me a receipt? – Tha borouses na mou dosis mia apodiksi?
Θα μπορούσες να μου δώσεις μια απόδειξη

You have been very nice – Isoun poli kalos
Ήσουν πολύ καλός

We had a very pleasant stay – Ichame mia efharisti diamoni
Είχαμε μια ευχάριστη διαμονή

We will definitely come back – Tha erthoume xana
Θα έρθουμε ξανά

PART XIV

CAMPING

► **Click Here for the .mp3 Audio**

Where is a camping site? – Pou boro na vro ena camping?
Που μπορώ να βρω ένα κάμπινγκ

Is there room for a tent? – Iparchi choros gia mia skini?
Υπάρχει χώρος για μια σκηνή

How much does one night cost? – Poso kostizi i diamoni gia ena vradi?
Πόσο κοστίζει η διαμονή για ένα βράδυ

How much does it cost for the car? – Poso kostizi na valo to amaxi mesa?
Πόσο κοστίζει να βάλω το αμάξι μέσα

Is there an electrical connection? – Iparchi ilektriko revma?
   Υπάρχει ηλεκτρικό ρεύμα

Is there room for another tent? – Iparchi choros kai gia mia akomi skini?
   Υπάρχει χώρος και για μια ακόμη σκηνή

Is there a shop here? – Iparchi magazi mesa?
   Υπάρχει μαγαζί μέσα

Is it safe to camp here? – Ine asfales na kataskinosoume edo?
   Είναι ασφαλές να κατασκηνώσουμε εδώ

What kind of animals are there around here? – Ti idous zoa kikloforoun edo?
   Τι είδους ζώα κυκλοφορούν εδώ

Where can I make a camp fire? – Pou boro na anapso mia ipethria fotia?
   Που μπορώ να ανάψω μια υπαίθρια φωτιά

Where are the restrooms? – Pou ine i toualetes?
   Που είναι οι τουαλέτες

PART XV

RESTAURANTS

► **Click Here for the .mp3 Audio**

Where is a good restaurant? – Pou boro na vro ena kalo estiatorio?
 Που μπορώ να βρω ένα καλό εστιατόριο

What time does the restaurant open? – Ti ora anigi to estiatorio?
 Τι ώρα ανοίγει το εστιατόριο

What time does the restaurant close? – Ti ora klini to estiatorio?
 Τι ώρα κλείνει το εστιατόριο

Where is a fast food place? – Pou boro na vro ena fast-foudadiko?
 Που μπορώ να βρω ένα φαστ-φουντάδικο

Where is a coffee shop? – Pou boro na vro mia cafeteria?
 Που μπορώ να βρω μια καφετέρια

Could you recommend me a restaurant? – Tha borouses na mou protinis ena estiatorio?
    Θα μπορούσες να μου προτείνεις ένα εστιατόριο

I am hungry – Pinao
    Πεινάω

I am thirsty – Dipsao
    Διψάω

I would like to reserve a table for (number) – Tha ithela na kliso ena trapezi gia (arithmos)
    Θα ήθελα να κλείσω ένα τραπέζι για (αριθμός)

I have a reservation – Echo kani kratisi
    Έχω κάνει κράτηση

I don't have a reservation – Den echo kratisi
    Δεν έχω κράτηση

Under whose name? – Se pio onoma?
    Σε ποιο όνομα

Can I get a table for (number)? – Boro na echo ena trapezi gia (arithmos)?
    Μπορώ να έχω ένα τραπέζι για (αριθμός)

How long do we have to wait? – Poso prepi na perimenoume?
    Πόσο πρέπει να περιμένουμε

Could you show me the menu? – Tha borousa na do ton katalogo?
Θα μπορούσα να δω τον κατάλογο

Could you show me the wine list? – Tha borousa na do ti krasia echete?
Θα μπορούσα να δω τι κρασιά έχετε

Waiter, we're ready to order – Servitore, imaste etimi na paraggiloume.
Σερβιτόρε, είμαστε έτοιμοι να παραγγείλουμε

What type of food do you have? – Ti fagita echete?
Τι φαγητά έχετε

What do you recommend? – Ti protinis?
Τι προτείνεις

What is the special for today? – Pio ine to piato tis imeras?
Ποιο είναι το πιάτο της ημέρας

What does it come with? – Me ti to servirete?
Με τι το σερβίρετε

What ingredients does it have? – Pos to ftiachnete?
Πως το φτιάχνετε

I would like to order (food) – Tha ithela na paraggilo (fagito)
Θα ήθελα να παραγγείλω (φαγητό)

I would like the meat under cooked – Tha ithela to kreas ligo psimeno

Θα ήθελα το κρέας λίγο ψημένο

I would like the meat half cooked – Tha ithela to kreas misopsimeno

Θα ήθελα το κρέας μισοψημένο

I would like the meat well cooked – Tha ithela to kreas poli kala psimeno

Θα ήθελα το κρέας πολύ καλά ψημένο

Is there a house specialty? – Iparchi kapia spesialite?

Υπάρχει κάποια σπεσιαλιτέ

Can I have a glass of water? – Boro na echo ena potiri nero?

Μπορώ να έχω ένα ποτήρι νερό

It is spicy? – Ine pikantiko?

Είναι πικάντικο

What would you recommend for desert? – Ti tha protines gia epidorpio?

Τι θα πρότεινες για επιδόρπιο

I am sorry, we currently don't have that – Lipame, den to echoume afti ti stigma

Λυπάμαι, δεν το έχουμε αυτή τη στιγμή

Would you like me to take the plates now? – Thelete na paro ta piata sas tora?

Θέλετε να πάρω τα πιάτα σας τώρα

Can I have the bill please? – Boro na echo to logariasmo parakalo?
Μπορώ να έχω το λογαριασμό παρακαλώ

I think there is a mistake on the bill – Nomizo echi ginei kapio lathos sto logariasmo
Νομίζω έχει γίνει κάποιο λάθος στο λογαριασμό

The food was excellent – To fagito itan iperocho
Το φαγητό ήταν υπέροχο

The service was excellent – I exipiretisi itan telia
Η εξυπηρέτηση ήταν τέλεια

Can I pay with a credit card? – Boro na pliroso me pistotiki?
Μπορώ να πληρώσω με πιστωτική

Keep the change – Krata ta resta
Κράτα τα ρέστα

What is there to eat? – Ti echi na fame?
Τι έχει να φάμε

What is there to drink? – Ti echi na pioume?
Τι έχει να πιούμε

I would like to order a delivery – Tha ithela na paro paketo gia to spiti
Θα ήθελα να πάρω πακέτο για το σπίτι

I am a vegetarian – Ime chortofagos
  Είμαι χορτοφάγος

PART XVI

POOL & BEACH

► **Click Here for the .mp3 Audio**

Where is the nearest beach? – Pou ine i pio kontini paralia?
   Που είναι η πιο κοντινή παραλία

Can we swim here? – Boroume na kolimpisoume edo?
   Μπορούμε να κολυμπήσουμε εδώ

What time is high tide? – Ti ora ine i paliria?
   Τι ώρα είναι η παλίρροια

What time is low tide? – Ti ora ine i aboti?
   Τι ώρα είναι η άμπωτη

Are there any strong currents? – Iparchoun dinata revmata?
   Υπάρχουν δυνατά ρεύματα

Where is a pool? – Pou boro na vro mia pisina?
  Που μπορώ να βρω μια πισίνα

How deep is the water? – Poso vathia ine?
  Πόσο βαθιά είναι

What time does the pool open? – Ti ora anigi i pisina?
  Τι ώρα ανοίγει η πισίνα

What time does the pool close? – Ti ora klini i pisina?
  Τι ώρα κλείνει η πισίνα

Is there a lifeguard? – Iparchi navagosostis?
  Υπάρχει ναυαγοσώστης

Is it safe for children? – Ine asfales gia ta pedia?
  Είναι ασφαλές για τα παιδιά

Where can I buy swimwear? – Apo pou boro na agoraso magio?
  Από πού μπορώ να αγοράσω μαγιό

Where is the kid's pool? – Pou ine i pediki pisina?
  Που είναι η παιδική πισίνα

Where can I park my car? – Pou boro na parkaro to amaxi?
  Που μπορώ να παρκάρω το αμάξι

Do I need a license to fish? – Chriazome adia gia na psarepso?
  Χρειάζομαι άδεια για να ψαρέψω;

PART XVII

NIGHTLIFE

► **Click Here for the .mp3 Audio**

Where is a good bar? – Pou boro na vro ena kalo bar?
  Που μπορώ να βρω ένα καλό μπαρ

What time does the business open? – Ti ora anigi i epichirisi?
  Τι ώρα ανοίγει η επιχείρηση

What time does the business close? – Ti ora klini i epichirisi?
  Τι ώρα κλείνει η επιχείρηση

Where is a good nightclub? – Pou boro na vro ena kalo club?
  Που μπορώ να βρω ένα καλό κλαμπ

Can I please have a (drink)? – Boro na echo ena (poto)?
  Μπορώ να έχω ένα (ποτό)

What kind of music do they put here? – Ti mousiki pezoun edo?
   Τι μουσική παίζουν εδώ

Would you like to dance? – Tha itheles na chorepsoume?
   Θα ήθελες να χορέψουμε

Where is the bathroom? – Pou ine i toualetes?
   Που είναι οι τουαλέτες

Could we dance here? – Boroume na chorepsoume edo?
   Μπορούμε να χορέψουμε εδώ

Do you serve alcohol here? – Servirete alkool?
   Σερβίρετε αλκοόλ

Do you put sport games on here? – Echete athlitika kanalia?
   Έχετε αθλητικά κανάλια;

PART XVIII

CINEMA

► **Click Here for the .mp3 Audio**

Where is a movie theatre? – Pou iparchi kinimatografos?
   Που υπάρχει κινηματογράφος

What time does the movie theatre open? – Ti ora anigi o kinimatografos?
   Τι ώρα ανοίγει ο κινηματογράφος

What time does the movie theatre close? – Ti ora klini o kinimatografos?
   Τι ώρα κλείνει ο κινηματογράφος

Which movies are they showing? – Pies tenies pezoun?
   Ποιες ταινίες παίζουν

Which movie do you recommend? – Pia tenia protinis?
   Ποια ταινία προτείνεις

What is the movie about? – Ti thema echi i tenia?
   Τι θέμα έχει η ταινία

Does the movie have good ratings? – Echi kales kritikes i tenia?
   Έχει καλές κριτικές η ταινία

How much does the ticket cost? – Poso kani to isitirio?
   Πόσο κάνει το εισιτήριο

Can I have a ticket for (movie)? – Boro na echo ena isitirio gia tin tenia (tenia)?
   Μπορώ να έχω ένα εισιτήριο για την ταινία (ταινία)
   Can I have a low seat? – Boro na echo mia thesi brosta?
   Μπορώ να έχω μια θέση μπροστά

Can I have a high seat? – Boro na echo mia thesi piso?
   Μπορώ να έχω μια θέση πίσω

Can I have a small popcorn? – Boro na echo ena mikro popcorn?
   Μπορώ να έχω ένα μικρό ποπκορν

Can I have a medium popcorn? – Boro na echo ena popcorn meseou megethous?
   Μπορώ να έχω ένα ποπκορν μεσαίου μεγέθους

Can I have a large popcorn? - Boro na echo ena megalo popcorn?
   Μπορώ να έχω ένα μεγάλο ποπκορν

74

Can I have a soda? – Boro na echo mia soda?
   Μπορώ να έχω μια σόδα

Can I have a hot dog? – Boro na echo ena hot dog?
   Μπορώ να έχω ένα hot dog

Can I have a hamburger? – Boro na echo ena hamburger?
   Μπορώ να έχω ένα hamburger

PART XIX

MUSEUM

► **Click Here for the .mp3 Audio**

Where is the (name) museum? – Pou ine to mousio (onoma)?
   Που είναι το μουσείο (όνομα)

How much is the entrance? – Poso echi i isodos?
   Πόσο έχει η είσοδος

What is the museum about? – Ti thema echi to mousio?
   Τι θέμα έχει το μουσείο

Is there a tour guide? – Iparchi xenagos?
   Υπάρχει ξεναγός

Where is the gift shop? – Pou ine to magazi me ta dora?
   Που είναι το μαγάζι με τα δώρα

Whose work is that? – Pianou ergo ine afto?
Ποιανού έργο είναι αυτό

Can I have a museum map? – Boro na echo ena charti tou mousiou?
Μπορώ να έχω ένα χάρτη του μουσείου

What time does the museum open? – Ti ora anigi to mousio?
Τι ώρα ανοίγει το μουσείο

What time does the museum close? – Ti ora klini to mousio?
Τι ώρα κλείνει το μουσείο

Can I take pictures? – Boro na travixo fotografies?
Μπορώ να τραβήξω φωτογραφίες

PART XX

SPORTING EVENTS

► **Click Here for the .mp3 Audio**

Where is the stadium? – Pou ine to stadio?
   Που είναι το στάδιο

What time does the stadium open? – Ti ora anigi to stadio?
   Τι ώρα ανοίγει το στάδιο

What time does the stadium close? - Ti ora klini to stadio?
   Τι ώρα κλείνει το στάδιο

What time is the game? – Ti ora ine o agonas?
   Τι ώρα είναι ο αγώνας

What time does the game end? – Ti ora telioni o agonas?
   Τι ώρα τελειώνει ο αγώνας

I would like to reserve tickets – Tha ithela na kliso isitiria
Θα ήθελα να κλείσω εισιτήρια

Where can I buy a ticket? – Apo pou boro na agoraso isitirio?
Από πού μπορώ να αγοράσω εισιτήριο

How much does the ticket cost? – Poso kani to isitirio?
Πόσο κάνει το εισιτήριο

I would like to buy a ticket – Tha ithela na agoraso ena isitirio
Θα ήθελα να αγοράσω ένα εισιτήριο

Where can I play (sport)? – Pou boro na pexo (athlima)?
Που μπορώ να παίξω (άθλημα)

Can I get a low seat? – Boro na echo mia thesi brosta?
Μπορώ να έχω μια θέση μπροστά

Can I get a high seat? – Boro na echo mia thesi piso?
Μπορώ να έχω μια θέση πίσω

Which team is winning the game? – Pia omada kerdizi? / Pios kerdizi?
Ποια ομάδα κερδίζει; / Ποιος κερδίζει

Which is your favorite team? – Pia ine i agapimeni sou omada?
Ποια είναι η αγαπημένη σου ομάδα

Which is your favorite sport? – Pio ine to agapimeno sou athlima?
Ποιο είναι το αγαπημένο σου άθλημα

When is the next game? – Pote ine to epomeno pechnidi?
 Πότε είναι το επόμενο παιχνίδι

Who won? – Pios kerdise?
 Ποιος κέρδισε;

PART XXI

SIGHTSEEING

► **Click Here for the .mp3 Audio**

What are the best places to go see in the city? – Pia ine ta kalitera meri na dis stin poli?
    Ποια είναι τα καλύτερα μέρη να δεις στην πόλη

Where is the zoo? – Pou ine o zoologikos kipos?
    Που είναι ο ζωολογικός κήπος

Where is the museum? – Pou ine to mousio?
    Που είναι το μουσείο

Where is the aquarium? – Pou ine to enidrio?
    Που είναι το ενυδρείο

Which are the oldest cathedrals? – Pioi ine i palioteri kathedriki nai?

81

Ποιοι είναι οι παλιότεροι καθεδρικοί ναοί

Where are the parks? – Pou ine to parko?
   Που είναι το πάρκο

Where can I find a travel guide? – Pou boro na vro xenago?
   Που μπορώ να βρω ξεναγό

Where is a tourism office? – Pou ine to grafio tourismou?
   Που είναι το γραφείο τουρισμού

Are there any tours in the city? – Ginonte xenagisis stin poli?
   Γίνονται ξεναγήσεις στην πόλη

How much does the tour cost? – Poso stichizi i xenagisi?
   Πόσο στοιχίζει η ξενάγηση

When does the tour start? – Pote archizi i xenagisi?
   Πότε αρχίζει η ξενάγηση

When does the tour end? - Pote telioni i xenagisi?
   Πότε τελειώνει η ξενάγηση

I need a guide that speaks English – Chriazome ena xenago pou milai Agglika
   Χρειάζομαι ένα ξεναγό που μιλάει Αγγλικά

Which are the places of interest? – Pia ine ta pio endiaferonta simia?
   Ποια είναι τα πιο ενδιαφέροντα σημεία

Do you have any brochures? – Echete filadia?
Έχετε φυλλάδια

Can I take pictures? – Boro na travixo fotografies?
Μπορώ να τραβήξω φωτογραφίες

Can I go in? – Boro na bo?
Μπορώ να μπω

Are we allowed to touch? – Boroume na aggixoume?
Μπορούμε να αγγίξουμε

What is that sculpture? – Ti dichni afto to glipto?
Τι δείχνει αυτό το γλυπτό

What is that painting? – Ti dichni aftos o pinakas?
Τι δείχνει αυτός ο πίνακας

What is that building? – Ti ine afto to ktirio?
Τι είναι αυτό το κτίριο

When was the sculpture made? – Pote egine to glipto?
Πότε έγινε το γλυπτό

When was the painting made? – Pote egine o pinakas?
Πότε έγινε ο πίνακας

When was the building made? – Pote chtistike to ktirio?
Πότε χτίστηκε το κτίριο

Where can I buy souvenirs? – Apo pou boro na agoraso souvenir?
   Από πού μπορώ να αγοράσω σουβενίρ;

PART XXII

BUSINESS

► **Click Here for the .mp3 Audio**

Where is the (name) company offices? – Pou ine ta grafia tis (onoma eterias)?
  Που είναι τα γραφεί της (όνομα εταιρείας)

I am on a business trip – Vriskome se epaggelmatiko taxidi
  Βρίσκομαι σε επαγγελματικό ταξίδι

I am looking for (name) – Psachno gia ton/tin (onoma)
  Ψάχνω για τον/την (όνομα)

I have an appointment with (name) – Echo radevou me ton/tin (onoma)
  Έχω ραντεβού με τον/την (όνομα)

I have a meeting with (name) – Echo sinantisi me ton/tin (onoma)
Έχω συνάντηση με τον/την (όνομα)

I am here for the conference – Irtha gia to sinedrio
Ήρθα για το συνέδριο

I am going to need an interpreter – Tha chriasto dierminea
Θα χρειαστώ διερμηνέα

I am here on official business – Vriskome edo gia epaggelmatikous logous
Βρίσκομαι εδώ για επαγγελματικούς λόγους

Where is (name)'s office? – Pou ine to grafio tou/tis (onoma)?
Που είναι το γραφείο του/της (όνομα)

The meeting will start at (time) – To meeting tha archisi stis (ora)
Το meeting θα αρχίσει στις (ώρα)

Where are the stairs? – Pou ine i skales?
Που είναι οι σκάλες

Where is the elevator? – Pou ine to asanser?
Που είναι το ασανσέρ

Sorry I am late – Signomi pou argisa
Συγγνώμη που άργησα

We have a new contract with the company – Ipograpsame kenourio simvoleo me tin eteria

Υπογράψαμε καινούριο συμβόλαιο με την εταιρεία

We had a board meeting – Ichame siskepsi
  Είχαμε σύσκεψη

The chairman of the board made a decision – O proedros pire mia apofasi
  Ο πρόεδρος πήρα μια απόφαση

The shareholders had a meeting – I metochi kanane siskepsi
  Οι μέτοχοι κάνανε σύσκεψη

We do business with the Chinese – Sinergazomaste me tous Kinezous
  Συνεργαζόμαστε με τους Κινέζους

We do business with the Japanese – Sinergazomaste me tous Iaponezous
  Συνεργαζόμαστε με τους Ιαπωνέζους

We do business with (country) – Sinergazomaste me tin (chora)
  Συνεργαζόμαστε με τη (χώρα)

The market has decreased – I agora echi pesi
  Η αγορά έχει πέσει

The market has increased – I agora echi anevi
  Η αγορά έχει ανέβει

The number of total workers has decreased to (number) – O sinolikos arithmos ton ergazomenon echi miothi se (arithmos)
  Ο συνολικός αριθμός των εργαζομένων έχει μειωθεί σε (αριθμός)

The number of total workers has reached (number) – O sinolikos arithmos ton ergazomenon echi ftasi tous (arithmos)
  Ο συνολικός αριθμός των εργαζομένων έχει φτάσει τους (αριθμός)

We have hired new personnel – Proslavame kenourio prosopiko
  Προσλάβαμε καινούριο προσωπικό

They came to an agreement – Irthan se simfonia
  Ήρθαν σε συμφωνία

They didn't come to an agreement – Den irthan se simfonia
  Δεν ήρθαν σε συμφωνία

We need to increase the prices by (number) percent – Prepi na afkisoume tis times kata (arithmos) tis ekato
  Πρέπει να αυξήσουμε τις τιμές κατά (αριθμός) τοις εκατό

We need to decrease the prices by (number) percent – Prepi na miosoume tis times kata (arithmos) tis ekato
  Πρέπει να μειώσουμε τις τιμές κατά (αριθμός) τοις εκατό

The profit margin went up (number) percent – To perithorio kerdous anevike (arithmos) tis ekato
  Το περιθώριο κέρδους ανέβηκε (αριθμός) τοις εκατό

The profit margin went down (number) percent – To perithorio kerdous katevike (arithmos) tis ekato
   Το περιθώριο κέρδους κατέβηκε (αριθμός) τοις εκατό

The total profit was (number) dollars – To sinoliko kerdos itan (arithmos) dolaria
   Το συνολικό κέρδος ήταν (αριθμός) δολάρια

The fiscal year will start on (date) – To dimosionomiko etos tha archisi stis (imerominia)
   Το δημοσιονομικό έτος θα αρχίσει στις (ημερομηνία)

The fiscal year will end on (date) – To dimosionomiko etos tha teliosi stis (imerominia)
   Το δημοσιονομικό έτος θα τελειώσει στις (ημερομηνία)

The stock market has decreased – To chrimatistirio epese
   Το χρηματιστήριο έπεσε

The stock market has increased – To chrimatistirio iche anodo
   Το χρηματιστήριο είχε άνοδο

We must decrease our market share – Prepi na miosoume tis polisis
   Πρέπει να μειώσουμε τις πωλήσεις
   We must increase our market share – Prepi na afksisoume tis polisis
   Πρέπει να αυξήσουμε τις πωλήσεις

We have a presentation to show – Echoume na kanoume mia parousiasi
   Έχουμε να κάνουμε μια παρουσίαση

In the presentation we will use graphs and statistics – Stin parousiasi tha chrisimopiisoume diagrammata kai statistika
Στην παρουσίαση θα χρησιμοποιήσουμε διαγράμματα και στατιστικά

This is a management level decision – Afti ine mia apofasi pou prepi na pari i diikisi
Αυτή είναι μια απόφαση που πρέπει να πάρει η διοίκηση

We were welcomed by the top management personnel in the company – Mas ipodechtike to diikitiko prosopiko tis eterias
Μας υποδέχτηκε το διοικητικό προσωπικό της εταιρείας

We need to find an advisor – Prepi na vroume enan simvoulo
Πρέπει να βρούμε έναν σύμβουλο

He is an external consultant – Ine exoterikos simvoulos
Είναι εξωτερικός σύμβουλος

I was promoted to (position) – Pira proagogi. Egina (thesi)
Πήρα προαγωγή. Έγινα (θέση)

It is difficult to find a good assistant – Ine diskolo na vris enan kalo voitho
Είναι δύσκολο να βρεις έναν καλό βοηθό

I need to find a good secretary – Prepi na vro mia kali gramatea
Πρέπει να βρω μια καλή γραμματέα

I am looking for a job – Psachno gia doulia

Ψάχνω για δουλειά

PART XXIII

SHOPPING

► **Click Here for the .mp3 Audio**

Where is the mall at? – Pou vriskete to eboriko?
Που βρίσκεται το εμπορικό

What time does the mall open? – Ti ora anigi to eboriko?
Τι ώρα ανοίγει το εμπορικό

What time does the mall close? - Ti ora klini to eboriko?
Τι ώρα κλείνει το εμπορικό

Where is the elevator? – Pou ine to asanser?
Που είναι το ασανσέρ

How much does this cost? – Poso kani?
Πόσο κάνει

Do you take American dollars? – Decheste dolaria Amerikis?
Δέχεστε δολάρια Αμερικής

Do you have something cheaper? – Echete kati pio ftino?
Έχετε κάτι πιο φθηνό

I would like to try this on – Tha ithela na to dokimaso afto
Θα ήθελα να το δοκιμάσω αυτό

Where are the changing rooms? – Pou ine ta dokimastiria?
Που είναι τα δοκιμαστήρια

Can you help me? – Boris na me voithisis?
Μπορείς να με βοηθήσεις

Is there anything I can help you with? – Boro na se voithiso?
Μπορώ να σε βοηθήσω

I am just looking – Apla kitazo
Απλά κοιτάζω

Could you show me (item)? – Tha borouses na mou diksis (pragma)?
Θα μπορούσες να μου δείξεις (πράγμα)

Do you have this in a small size? – To echete se mikro megethos?
Το έχετε σε μικρό μέγεθος

Do you have this in a medium size? - To echete se meseo megethos?

Το έχετε σε μεσαίο μέγεθος

Do you have this in a large size? - To echete se megalo megethos?
Το έχετε σε μεγάλο μέγεθος

What time does the store open? – Ti ora anigi to magazi?
Τι ώρα ανοίγει το μαγαζί

What time does the store close? - Ti ora klini to magazi?
Τι ώρα κλείνει το μαγαζί

Do you have this in a different color? – To echis se allo chroma?
Το έχεις σε άλλο χρώμα

Do you have any more of these? – Echis ki alla apo afta?
Έχεις και άλλα από αυτά

Where do I pay? – Pou plirono?
Που πληρώνω

What guarantee does this have? – Ti eggiisi echi?
Τι εγγύηση έχει

Do you need anything else? – Chriazese kati allo?
Χρειάζεσαι κάτι άλλο

That's all – Afta icha
Αυτά είχα

Where can I buy clothes for men? – Apo pou boro na agoraso roucha gia andres?

Από πού μπορώ να αγοράσω ρούχα για άνδρες

Where can I buy clothes for women? – Apo pou boro na agoraso ginekia roucha?

Από πού μπορώ να αγοράσω γυναικεία ρούχα

Where can I buy clothes for kids? – Apo pou boro na agoraso paidika roucha?

Από πού μπορώ να αγοράσω παιδικά ρούχα

Where can I buy clothes for babies? – Apo pou boro na agoraso vrefika roucha?

Από πού μπορώ να αγοράσω βρεφικά ρούχα

Where can I buy shoes? – Apo pou boro na agoraso papoutsia?

Από πού μπορώ να αγοράσω παπούτσια

Where are the bathrooms? – Pou ine i toualetes?

Που είναι οι τουαλέτες

Where is the food section? – Pou ine ta fagadika?

Που είναι τα φαγάδικα

PART XXIV

SUPERMARKET

► **Click Here for the .mp3 Audio**

Where is the nearest supermarket? – Pou ine to pio kontino supermarket?

Που είναι το πιο κοντινό σούπερ μάρκετ

Where is the nearest grocery store? - Pou ine to pio kontino manaviko?

Που είναι το πιο κοντινό μανάβικο

What time does the supermarket open? – Ti ora anigi to supermarket?

Τι ώρα ανοίγει το σούπερ μάρκετ

What time does the supermarket close? - Ti ora klini to supermarket?

Τι ώρα κλείνει το σούπερ μάρκετ

Where is the fruit and vegetable section? – Pou ine to tmima manavikis?
Που είναι το τμήμα μαναβικής

Where is the dairy section? – Pou ine o diadromos me ta galaktokomika?
Που είναι ο διάδρομος με τα γαλακτοκομικά

Where is the grain section? – Pou ine o diadromos me ta dimitriaka?
Που είναι ο διάδρομος με τα δημητριακά

Where is the beverage section? – Pou ine o diadromos me ta pota?
Που είναι ο διάδρομος με τα ποτά

Where is the frozen food section? – Pou ine o diadromos me ta katepsigmena?
Που είναι ο διάδρομος με τα κατεψυγμένα

Where is the hygiene section? – Pou ine o diadromos me ta idi prosopikis igiinis?
Που είναι ο διάδρομος με τα είδη προσωπικής υγιεινής;

How much is a kilo of (product)? – Poso kani ena kilo (proion)?
Πόσο κάνει ένα κιλό (προϊόν)

I need (number) kilos/pounds of that – Thelo (arithmos) kila apo afto.
Θέλω (αριθμός) κιλά από αυτό

Where do I pay? – Pou plirono?
Που πληρώνω

How much is the total? – Poso ine sto sinolo?
Πόσο είναι στο σύνολο

Where is the butcher shop? – Pou ine to kreopolio?
Που είναι το κρεοπωλείο

Where is the bakery? – Pou ine o fournos?
Που είναι ο φούρνος

Do you make deliveries? – Kanete paradosis sto spiti?
Κάνετε παραδόσεις στο σπίτι

What is the supermarket's number? – Pio ine to tilefono tou supermarket?
Ποιο είναι το τηλέφωνο του σούπερ μάρκετ

PART XXV

FRUITS & VEGETABLES

► **Click Here for the .mp3 Audio**

Do you have any (name)? – Echis katholou (onoma)?
Έχεις καθόλου (όνομα)

Could you give me a kilo of (name)? – Tha borouses na mou dosis ena kilo (onoma)?
Θα μπορούσες να μου δώσεις ένα κιλό (όνομα)

Could you give me a pound of (name)? – (Note: pound is not used in Greece.)

Fruits – Frouta
Φρούτα

Apples – mila

Μήλα

Avocados – avocado
   Αβοκάντο

Blackberries – moura
   Μούρα

Cherries – kerasia
   Κεράσια

Grapes – stafilia
   Σταφύλια

Oranges – portokalia
   Πορτοκάλια

Strawberries – fraoules
   Φράουλες

Bananas – bananes
   Μπανάνες

Mangos – mango
   Μάνγκο
   Guavas – guava
   Γκουάβα

Lemons – lemonia
   Λεμόνια

Limes – lime
Λάιμ

Pears – achladia
Αχλάδια

Pineapples – Ananas
Ανανάς

Watermelons – karpouzia
Καρπούζια

Vegetables – lachanika
Λαχανικά

Beans – fasolia
Φασόλια

Broccoli – mprokola
Μπρόκολα

Carrots – karota
Καρότα

Garlic – skordo
Σκόρδο

Lettuce – marouli
Μαρούλι

Mushrooms – manitaria
   Μανιτάρια

Onion – kremidi
   Κρεμμύδι

Peas – arakas
   Αρακάς

Potatoe – patata
   Πατάτα

Pumkins – Kolokithes
   Κολοκύθες

Tomatos – tomates
   Ντομάτες

Yam – glikopatata
   Γλυκοπατάτα

PART XXVI

HOSPITAL, DOCTOR'S OFFICE, & DENTIST

► **Click Here for the .mp3 Audio**

Where is the nearest hospital? – Pou ine to pio kontino nosokomio?
  Που είναι το πιο κοντινό νοσοκομείο

Where is the hospital (name)? – Pou ine to nosokomio (onoma)?
  Που είναι το νοσοκομείο (όνομα)

Is there a doctor who speaks English? – Iparchi kapoios giatros pou milai Agglika?
  Υπάρχει κάποιος γιατρός που μιλάει Αγγλικά

I don't have health insurance – Den echo asfalia igias
  Δεν έχω ασφάλεια υγείας

Please wait a moment – Perimenete ligo

Περιμένετε λίγο

What is the name of the patient? – Pio ine to onoma tou astheni?
Ποιο είναι το όνομα του ασθενή

Please fill out this document – Parakalo simpliroste afto to entipo
Παρακαλώ συμπληρώστε αυτό το έντυπο

What is your address? – Pia ine i diefthinsi sou?
Ποια είναι η διεύθυνση σου

Can I have a phone number in case of an emergency? – Boro na echo ena tilefono se periptosi anagkis?
Μπορώ να έχω ένα τηλέφωνο σε περίπτωση ανάγκης

Please take a seat and wait to be called – Kathiste parakalo kai perimenete na sas kalesoun
Καθίστε παρακαλώ και περιμένετε να σας καλέσουν

Can I see your identification? – Boro na do tin taftotita sou?
Μπορώ να δω την ταυτότητα σου

I have an appointment at (time) with Dr. (name) – Echo radevou stis (ora) me ton giatro (onoma)
Έχω ραντεβού στις (ώρα) με το γιατρό (όνομα)

What brings you here? – Ti se ferni edo?
Τι σε φέρνει εδώ

I feel very sick – Niotho chalia / Ime poli arostos

Νιώθω χάλια / Είμαι πολύ άρρωστος

I have a headache – Echo ponokefalo
Έχω πονοκέφαλο

I have a stomach ache – Me ponai i kilia
Με πονάει η κοιλιά

I have a fever – Echo pireto
Έχω πυρετό

I feel nauseous – Echo tasi pros emeto
Έχω τάση προς εμετό

I feel a lot of pain – Ponao poli
Πονάω πολύ

Are you allergic to any medicine? – Ise alergikos se kapio farmako?
Είσαι αλλεργικός σε κάποιο φάρμακο

Have you taken any medication? – Ise se farmakeftiki agogi?
Είσαι σε φαρμακευτική αγωγή

Do you smoke, drink alcohol, or use drugs? – Kapnizis, pinis i kanis chrisi apagorevmenon ousion?
Καπνίζεις, πίνεις ή κάνεις χρήση απαγορευμένων ουσιών

Have you ever had surgery? – Echis kani pote eghirisi?
Έχεις κάνει ποτέ εγχείρηση

We are going to have to operate on you – Prepi na kanete eghirisi
Πρέπει να κάνετε εγχείρηση

What blood type are you? – Ti omada ematos echis?
Τι ομάδα αίματος έχεις

I am blood type (type) – I omada ematos mou ine (omada ematos)
Η ομάδα αίματος μου είναι (ομάδα αίματος)

I need to give you an injection – Prepi na sou kano enesi
Πρέπει να σου κάνω ένεση

I need a blood sample – Chriazome digma ematos
Χρειάζομαι δείγμα αίματος

I need a urine sample - Chriazome digma ouron
Χρειάζομαι δείγμα ούρων

I need you to take your clothes off – Prepi na vgalis ta roucha sou /
Prepi na ksentithis
Πρέπει να βγάλεις τα ρούχα σου / Πρέπει να ξεντυθείς

This is your prescription – Afta ine ta farmaka sou
Αυτά είναι τα φάρμακα σου

Take a pill every (number) hours – Na pernis ena chapi ana
(arithmos) ores
Να παίρνεις ένα χάπι ανά (αριθμός) ώρες

The next appointment is on (date) – To epomeno radevou mas ine stis (imerominia)

Το επόμενο ραντεβού μας είναι στις (ημερομηνία)

Where is the closest dentist? – Pou ine to pio kontino odontiatrio?

Που είναι το πιο κοντινό οδοντιατρείο

When was the last time you were at the dentist? – Pote piges teleftea fora ston odontiatro?

Πότε πήγες τελευταία φορά στον οδοντίατρο

Open your mouth as much as you can and keep it open – Anikse to stoma sou oso perissotero boris kai kratise to anichto

Άνοιξε το στόμα σου όσο περισσότερο μπορείς και κράτησε το ανοιχτό

I am going to use this instrument to touch some areas on your teeth – Tha chrisimopiiso afto to ergalio gia na aggixo kapia simia sta dontia sou

Θα χρησιμοποιήσω αυτό το εργαλείο για να αγγίξω κάποια σημεία στα δόντια σου

Does it hurt here? – Ponas edo?

Πονάς εδώ

You have some cavities that we must treat – Prepi na kanoume kapia sfragismata

Πρέπει να κάνουμε κάποια σφραγίσματα

Please call an ambulance – Kalese ena asthenoforo se parakalo

Κάλεσε ένα ασθενοφόρο σε παρακαλώ

PART XXVII

POLICE

► **Click Here for the .mp3 Audio**

Where is the nearest police station? – Pou ine to pio kontino astinomiko tmima?
Που είναι το πιο κοντινό αστυνομικό τμήμα

Please call the police – Se parakalo kalese tin astinomia
Σε παρακαλώ κάλεσε την αστυνομία

I came to report a theft – Thelo na anafero mia klopi
Θέλω να αναφέρω μια κλοπή

They stole my phone – Eklepsan to tilefono mou
Έκλεψαν το τηλέφωνο

They stole my wallet – Eklepsan to portofoli mou

Έκλεψαν το πορτοφόλι μου

I have received a threat – Me apiloun
Με απειλούν

Where did they steal your item? – Pou se klepsane?
Που σε κλέψανε

You must go to the police station – Prepi na pas sto astinomiko tmima
Πρέπει να πας στο αστυνομικό τμήμα

I need to call the police – Prepi na kaleso tin astinomia
Πρέπει να καλέσω την αστυνομία

I am an American citizen – Ime Amerikanos politis
Είμαι Αμερικανός πολίτης

I want to call the American Embassy – Thelo na kaleso tin Amerikaniki Presvia
Θέλω να καλέσω την Αμερικάνικη Πρεσβεία

I want to talk to a lawyer – Thelo na miliso se ena dikigoro
Θέλω να μιλήσω σε ένα δικηγόρο

PART XXVIII

PHARMACY

► **Click Here for the .mp3 Audio**

Where is the nearest pharmacy? – Pou ine to pio kontino farmakio?
Που είναι το πιο κοντινό φαρμακείο

What time does the pharmacy open? – Ti ora anigi to farmakio?
Τι ώρα ανοίγει το φαρμακείο

What time does the pharmacy close? – Ti ora klini to farmakio?
Τι ώρα κλείνει το φαρμακείο

I need this prescription – Chriazome afti ti sintagi / afta ta farmaka
Χρειάζομαι αυτή τη συνταγή / αυτά τα φάρμακα

Is this the first time you have visited our pharmacy? – Proti fora erchese sto farmakio mas?

Πρώτη φορά έρχεσαι στο φαρμακείο μας;

Can you give me something for my allergies? – Boris na mou dosis kati gia tin allergia mou?
  Μπορείς να μου δώσεις κάτι για την αλλεργία μου

How often do I take the medicine? – Poso sichna na perno to farmako?
  Πόσο συχνά να παίρνω το φάρμακο

I need this medicine – Chriazome afto to farmako
  Χρειάζομαι αυτό το φάρμακο

Can I pick the medicine up later? – Boro na ertho na paro to farmako argotera?
  Μπορώ να έρθω να πάρω το φάρμακο αργότερα

When can I pick it up? – Pote boro na ertho na to paro?
  Πότε μπορώ να έρθω να το πάρω

Can you tell me what medicine to take? – Boris na mou pis ti farmako na paro?
  Μπορείς να μου πεις τι φάρμακο να πάρω

What symptoms do you have? – Ti simptomata echis?
  Τι συμπτώματα έχεις

I have a headache – Echo ponokefalo
  Έχω πονοκέφαλο

I have a stomach ache – Echo ponokilo
Έχω πονόκοιλο

Do you have anything for mosquito bites? – Echete na mou dosete kati gia ta tsibimata apo ta kounoupia?
Έχετε να μου δώσετε κάτι για τα τσιμπήματα από τα κουνούπια

Do you have any mosquito repellent? – Echete kounoupeleo?
Έχετε κουνουπέλαιο

Do you have any sun block? – Echete antiliako?
Έχετε αντηλιακό

Do you have any tanning lotion? – Echete losion gia mavrisma?
Έχετε λοσιόν για μαύρισμα

Do you have rubbing alcohol? – Echete inopnevma entrivis?
Έχετε οινόπνευμα εντριβής

Do you have q-tips? – Echete batonetes?
Έχετε μπατονέτες

Do you have toothbrushes? – Echete odontovourtses?
Έχετε οδοντόβουρτσες

Do you have toothpaste? – Echete odontokrema?
Έχετε οδοντόκρεμα

Do you have soap? – Echete sapouni?
Έχετε σαπούνι

Do you have shampoo? – Echete sampouan?
   Έχετε σαμπουάν

Do you have body cream? – Echete krema gia to soma?
   Έχετε κρέμα για το σώμα

Do you have deodorant? – Echete aposmitiko?
   Έχετε αποσμητικό

Do you have perfume? – Echete aromata?
   Έχετε αρώματα

Where do I pay? – Pou plirono?
   Που πληρώνω;

PART XXIX

EMOTIONS

► **Click Here for the .mp3 Audio**

How are you feeling? – Pos esthanese?
   Πως αισθάνεσαι

I feel bad – Chalia
   Χάλια

I feel good – Kala
   Καλά

I feel dizzy – Zalismenos
   Ζαλισμένος

I feel sad – Lipimenos
   Λυπημένος

I feel happy – Charoumenos
   Χαρούμενος

I feel angry – Thimomenos
   Θυμωμένος

I feel scared – Fovismenos
   Φοβισμένος

I feel nervous – Aghomenos
   Αγχωμένος

I feel depressed – Niotho melagholia
   Νιώθω μελαγχολία

I like it – Mou aresi
   Μου αρέσει

I like him – Mou aresi / Ton simpatho
   Μου αρέσει / Τον συμπαθώ

I like her – Mou aresi / Ti simpatho
   Μου αρέσει / Την συμπαθώ

I don't like it – Den mou aresi
   Δεν μου αρέσει

I don't like him – Den mou aresi / Den ton simpatho
   Δεν μου αρέσει / Δεν τον συμπαθώ

I don't like her – Den mou aresi / Den tin simpatho
   Δεν μου αρέσει / Δεν την συμπαθώ

I love him – Ton agapao
   Τον αγαπάω

I love her – Tin agapao
   Την αγαπάω

PART XXX

EMERGENCIES

► <u>**Click Here for the .mp3 Audio**</u>

Help! – Voithia!
Βοήθεια!

It's an emergency – Ine epigon
Είναι επείγον

I have an emergency – Echo ena epigon peristatiko
Έχω ένα επείγον περιστατικό

Emergency Exit – Exodos kindinou
Έξοδος Κινδύνου

First Aid – Protes Voithies
Πρώτες Βοήθειες

I got hurt – Chtipisa
Χτύπησα

It hurts a lot – Ponai poli
Πονάει πολύ

Call the police – Pare tin astinomia
Πάρε την αστυνομία

Call an ambulance – Kalese ena asthenoforo
Κάλεσε ένα ασθενοφόρο

Call the fire department – Kalese tin pirosvestiki
Κάλεσε την πυροσβεστική

I felt an earthquake – Eniosa enan sismo
Ένιωσα έναν σεισμό

My passport has been stolen – Mou eklepsan to diavatirio
Μου έκλεψαν το διαβατήριο

My cellphone has been stolen – Mou eklepsan to kinito
Μου έκλεψαν το κινητό

My wallet has been stolen – Mou eklepsan to portofoli
Μου έκλεψαν το πορτοφόλι

Stop thief! – Stamata! Kleftis!
Σταμάτα! Κλέφτης!

The door is locked and I can't get out – I porta ine klidomeni kai de boro na vgo

Η πόρτα είναι κλειδωμένη και δε μπορώ να βγω

My blood type is (type) – I omada ematos mou ine (omada ematos)

Η ομάδα αίματος μου είναι (ομάδα αίματος)

Where is the emergency exit? – Pou ine i exodus kindinou?

Που είναι η έξοδος κινδύνου

I am having a heart attack – Patheno emfragma

Παθαίνω έμφραγμα

Please send help immediately – Sas parakalo stilte amesos voithia

Σας παρακαλώ στείλτε αμέσως βοήθεια

I am bleeding profusely – Matono ipervolika

Ματώνω υπερβολικά

I have been robbed – Me listepsan

Με λήστεψαν

PART XXXI

BANK

► **Click Here for the .mp3 Audio**

Where is the bank? – pou ine i trapeza?
  Που είναι η τράπεζα

Which is a good bank to open an account? – Se pia trapeza ine kalitera na anixo logariasmo?
  Σε ποια τράπεζα είναι καλύτερα να ανοίξω λογαριασμό

Where is the atm? – Pou ine to ATM?
  Που είναι το ATM

What time does the bank open? – Ti ora anigi i trapeza?
  Τι ώρα ανοίγει η τράπεζα

What time does the bank close? – Ti ora klini i trapeza?

Τι ώρα κλείνει η τράπεζα

Can I open an account? – Boro na anixo ena logariasmo?
Μπορώ να ανοίξω ένα λογαριασμό

This is my account number – Aftos ine o arithmos tou logariasmou mou
Αυτός είναι ο αριθμός του λογαριασμού μου

This is my passport – Afto ine to diavatirio mou
Αυτό είναι το διαβατήριο μου

This is my address – Afti ine i diefthinsi mou
Αυτή είναι η διεύθυνση μου

I need to talk to a consultant – Prepi na miliso se ena simvoulo
Πρέπει να μιλήσω σε ένα σύμβουλο

Can I make a loan? – Boro na paro danio?
Μπορώ να πάρω δάνειο

I would like to make a deposit – Tha ithela na kano mia katathesi
Θα ήθελα να κάνω μια κατάθεση

I would like to make a withdrawal – Tha ithela na kano mia analipsi
Θα ήθελα να κάνω μια ανάληψη

I would like to exchange this money – Tha ithela na antalaxo afta ta chrimata
Θα ήθελα να ανταλλάξω αυτά τα χρήματα

I need dollars – Chriazome dolaria
   Χρειάζομαι δολάρια

Could you give me small bills? – Tha borouses na mou dosis chartonomismata mikris axias?
   Θα μπορούσες να μου δώσεις χαρτονομίσματα μικρής αξίας

Could you give me large bills? – Tha borouses na mou dosis chartonomismata megalis axias?
   Θα μπορούσες να μου δώσεις χαρτονομίσματα μεγάλης αξίας

How much money can I withdraw from the atm? – Posa chrimata boro na travixo apo to ATM?
   Πόσα χρήματα μπορώ να τραβήξω από το ATM

I would like a bank statement – Tha ithela ena ekkatharistiko trapezikou logariasmou
   Θα ήθελα ένα εκκαθαριστικό τραπεζικού λογαριασμού

I would like to cash a traveler's check – Tha ithela na exargiroso mia taxidiotiki epitagi
   Θα ήθελα να εξαργυρώσω μια ταξιδιωτική επιταγή

I would like to get a credit card – Tha ithela na vgalo mia pistotiki karta
   Θα ήθελα να βγάλω μια πιστωτική κάρτα

I would like to get a debit card – Tha ithela na vgalo mia chreostiki karta
   Θα ήθελα να βγάλω μια χρεωστική κάρτα

Where do I have to sign? – Pou prepi na ipograpso?
Που πρέπει να υπογράψω

PART XXXII

POST OFFICE

► **Click Here for the .mp3 Audio**

Where is the post office? – Pou ine to tachidromio?
　　Που είναι το ταχυδρομείο

What time does the post office open? – Ti ora anigi to tachidromio?
　　Τι ώρα ανοίγει το ταχυδρομείο

What time does the post office close? - Ti ora klini to tachidromio?
　　Τι ώρα κλείνει το ταχυδρομείο

I would like to send a letter – Tha ithela na stilo ena gramma
　　Θα ήθελα να στείλω ένα γράμμα

I would like to send a package – Tha ithela na stilo ena dema
　　Θα ήθελα να στείλω ένα δέμα

I would like to send money – Tha ithela na stilo chrimata
Θα ήθελα να στείλω χρήματα

Is there any mail for me? – Iparchi kapio gramma gia mena?
Υπάρχει κάποιο γράμμα για μένα

How much is it? – Poso kani?
Πόσο κάνει

PART XXXIII

TECHNOLOGY

► **Click Here for the .mp3 Audio**

Is there an Internet café nearby? – Iparchi Internet café edo konta?
Υπάρχει internet café εδώ κοντά

Is there a computer available that I could use? – Iparchi kapios ipologistis pou na boro na chrisimopiiso?
Υπάρχει κάποιος υπολογιστής που να μπορώ να χρησιμοποιήσω

Use computer number (number) – Chrisimopiise ton ipologisti (arithmos)
Χρησιμοποίησε τον υπολογιστή (αριθμός)

I need to use the Internet – Prepi na chrisimopiiso to internet
Πρέπει να χρησιμοποιήσω το internet

I need to send an email – Prepi na stilo ena email
    Πρέπει να στείλω ένα email

I need to print something out – Prepi na ektiposo kati
    Πρέπει να εκτυπώσω κάτι

How do I print? – Pos ektipono?
    Πως εκτυπώνω

Which printer should I use? – Pio ektipoti na chrisimopiiso?
    Ποιον εκτυπωτή να χρησιμοποιήσω

I need to photo copy this – Prepi na to ektiposo se fotografia
    Πρέπει να το εκτυπώσω σε φωτογραφία

I need to scan this – prepi na to skanaro
    Πρέπει να το σκανάρω

I need to send this through fax – Prepi na to stilo me fax
    Πρέπει να το στείλω με φαξ

I need help – Chriazome voithia
    Χρειάζομαι βοήθεια

I forgot to save the file – xechasa na apothikefso to archio
    Ξέχασα να αποθηκεύσω το αρχείο

How much does (number) minutes on the computer cost? – Poso stichizoun (arithmos) lepta ston ipologisti?
    Πόσο στοιχίζουν (αριθμός) λεπτά στον υπολογιστή

I need to make a call to a cellphone – Prepi na tilefoniso se kinito
  Πρέπει να τηλεφωνήσω σε κινητό

I need to make a call to the United States – Prepi na kano ena tilefonima stin Ameriki
  Πρέπει να κάνω ένα τηλεφώνημα στην Αμερική

I need to make a call to Canada – Prepi na kano ena tilefonima ston Kanada
  Πρέπει να κάνω ένα τηλεφώνημα στον Καναδά

I need to make a call to Australia – Prepi na kano ena tilefonima stin Afstralia
  Πρέπει να κάνω ένα τηλεφώνημα στην Αυστραλία

I need to make a call to Europe – Prepi na kano ena tilefonima stin Evropi
  Πρέπει να κάνω ένα τηλεφώνημα στην Ευρώπη

How much does a minute to (place) cost? – Poso kostizi to lepto sto/sti (meros)?
  Πόσο κοστίζει το λεπτό στο/στη (μέρος)

How much do I owe you? – Posa sou chrostao?
  Πόσα σου χρωστάω

PART XXXIV

LAUNDRY

► **Click Here for the .mp3 Audio**

Where is the nearest laundromat? – Pou ine ta plisiestera plintiria kinis chrisis?
    Που είναι τα πλησιέστερα πλυντήρια κοινής χρήσης

What time does the laundromat open? – Ti ora anigoun ta plintiria kinis chrisis?
    Τι ώρα ανοίγουν τα πλυντήρια κοινής χρήσης

What time does the laundromat close? - Ti ora klinoun ta plintiria kinis chrisis?
    Τι ώρα κλείνουν τα πλυντήρια κοινής χρήσης

Where is a dry cleaner? – Pou iparchi katharistirio?
    Που υπάρχει καθαριστήριο

Can I leave these clothes and pick them up when they are ready? –
Boro na afiso afta ta roucha kai na ta paro otan tha ine etima?
Μπορώ να αφήσω αυτά τα ρούχα και να τα πάρω όταν θα είναι
έτοιμα

Could you dry the clothes? – Tha borouses na stegnosis ta roucha?
Θα μπορούσες να στεγνώσεις τα ρούχα

Could you fold the clothes? – Tha borouses na diplosis ta roucha?
Θα μπορούσες να διπλώσεις τα ρούχα

How much does it cost? – Poso kani?
Πόσο κάνει

How long will it take? – Posi ora tha pari?
Πόση ώρα θα πάρει

Which washing machine can I use? – pio plintirio boro na
chrisimopiiso?
Ποιο πλυντήριο μπορώ να χρησιμοποιήσω

Which dryer can I use? – Pio stegnotirio boro na chrisimopiiso?
Ποιο στεγνωτήριο μπορώ να χρησιμοποιήσω

Where can I fold my clothes? – Pou boro na diploso ta roucha mou?
Που μπορώ να διπλώσω τα ρούχα μου

Is there a basket I can use? – Iparchi kapio kalathi pou na boro na
chrisimopiiso?
Υπάρχει κάποιο καλάθι που να μπορώ να χρησιμοποιήσω

Do you have detergent? – Echis aporipantiko?
   Έχεις απορρυπαντικό

Do you have bleach? – Echis lefkantiko?
   Έχεις λευκαντικό

Do you have stain remover? – echis katharistiko gia lekedes?
   Έχεις καθαριστικό για λεκέδες

Do you have fabric softener? – Echis malaktiko?
   Έχεις μαλακτικό

Where do I pay? – pou plirono?
   Που πληρώνω

PART XXXV

MONEY

► **Click Here for the .mp3 Audio**

How much is it? – poso kani?
   Πόσο κάνει

How much do I owe you? – Posa sou chrostao?
   Πόσα σου χρωστάω

How much does this cost? – Poso kani afto?
   Πόσο κάνει αυτό

How much money will I need? – posa chrimata tha chriasto?
   Πόσα χρήματα θα χρειαστώ

I don't have money – Den echo chrimata
   Δεν έχω χρήματα

Where do I pay? – Pou plirono?
Που πληρώνω

Very cheap – Poli ftino
Πολύ φθηνό

Very expensive – Poli akrivo
Πολύ ακριβό

Do you have change for a (number) bill? – Echis na mou dosis psila gia ena chartonomisma (arithmos)?
Έχεις να μου δώσεις ψιλά για ένα χαρτονόμισμα (αριθμός)

Where can I change money? – Pou boro na antalaxo ta chrimata?
Που μπορώ να ανταλλάξω τα χρήματα

How much is the dollar worth? – Poso axizi to dolario?
Πόσο αξίζει το δολάριο

What is the exchange rate? – Pia ine i timi tou sinallagmatos?
Ποια είναι η τιμή του συναλλάγματος

Do you take credit card? – Decheste pistotikes?
Δέχεστε πιστωτικές

Keep the change – Krata ta resta
Κράτα τα ρέστα

Here is a tip – Oriste ena filodorima
Ορίστε ένα φιλοδώρημα

PART XXXVI

CARDINAL NUMBERS

► **Click Here for the .mp3 Audio**

0 - *Zero* – miden
   μηδέν

1 - *One* – ena
   ένα

2 - *Two* – dio
   δύο

3 - *Three* – tria
   Τρία

4 - *Four* – tessera
   τέσσερα

5 - *Five* – pente
πέντε

6 – *Six* – exi
έξι

7 – *Seven* – epta
επτά

8 – *Eight* – okto
οκτώ

9 – *Nine* – ennea
εννέα

10 – *Ten* – deka
δέκα

11 – *Eleven* – edeka
έντεκα

12 – *Twelve* – dodeka
δώδεκα

13 – *Thirteen* – dekatria
δεκατρία

14 – *Fourteen* – dekatessera
δεκατέσσερα

15 – *Fifteen* – dekapente
δεκαπέντε

16 – *Sixteen* – dekaexi
δεκαέξι

17 – *Seventeen* – dekaefta
δεκαεφτά

18 – *Eighteen* – dekaokto
δεκαοκτώ

19 – *Nineteen* – dekaenia
Δεκαεννιά

20 – *Twenty* – ikosi
είκοσι

21 – *Twenty-One* – ikosi ena
Είκοσι ένα

22 – *Twenty-Two* – ikosi dio
Είκοσι δύο

23 – *Twenty-Three* – ikosi tria
Είκοσι τρία

24 – *Twenty-Four* – ikosi tessera
Είκοσι τέσσερα

25 – *Twenty-Five* – ikosi pente
Είκοσι πέντε

26 – *Twenty-Six* – ikosi exi
Είκοσι έξι

27 – *Twenty-Seven* – ikosi epta
Είκοσι επτά

28 – *Twenty-Eight* – ikosi okto
Είκοσι οκτώ

29 – *Twenty-Nine* – ikosi ennia
Είκοσι εννιά

30 – *Thirty* – trianta
τριάντα

31 – *Thirty-One* – trianta ena
Τριάντα ένα

32 – *Thirty-Two* – trianta dio
Τριάντα δύο

33 – *Thirty-Three* – trianta tria
Τριάντα τρία

34 – *Thirty-Four* – trianta tessera
Τριάντα τέσσερα

35 – *Thirty-Five* – trianta pente
Τριάντα πέντε

36 – *Thirty-Six* – trianta exi
Τριάντα έξι

37 – *Thirty-Seven* – trianta epta
Τριάντα επτά

38 – *Thirty-Eight* – trianta okto
Τριάντα οκτώ

39 – *Thirty-Nine* – trianta ennia
Τριάντα εννιά

40 – *Forty* – saranta
σαράντα

45 – *Forty-Five* – saranta pente
Σαράντα πέντε

50 – *Fifty* – peninta
Πενήντα

60 – *Sixty* – exinta
Εξήντα

70 – *Seventy* – evdominta
Εβδομήντα

80 – *Eighty* – ogdonta
Ογδόντα

90 – *Ninety* – eneninta
Ενενήντα

100 – *One Hundred* – ekato
Εκατό

150 – *One Hundred Fifty* – ekato peninta
εκατό πενήντα

200 – *Two Hundred* – diakosia
Διακόσια

250 – *Two Hundred Fifty* – diakosia peninta
Διακόσια πενήντα

300 – *Three Hundred* – triakosia
Τριακόσια

400 – *Four Hundred* – tetrakosia
Τετρακόσια

500 – *Five Hundred* – pentakosia
Πεντακόσια

600 – *Six Hundred* – exakosia
Εξακόσια

700 – *Seven Hundred* – eptakosia
Επτακόσια

800 – *Eight Hundred* – oktakosia
Οκτακόσια

900 – *Nine Hundred* – eniakosia
Ενιακόσια

1000 – *One Thousand* – chilia
Χίλια

1500 - *One Thousand Five Hundred* – chilia pentakosia
Χίλια πεντακόσια

2000 – *Two Thousand* – dio chiliades
Δύο χιλιάδες

3000 – *Three Thousand* – tris chiliades
Τρεις χιλιάδες

4000 – *Four Thousand* – tesseris chiliades
Τέσσερις χιλιάδες

5000 – *Five Thousand* – pente chiliades
Πέντε χιλιάδες

6000 – *Six Thousand* – exi chiliades
Έξι χιλιάδες

7000 – *Seven Thousand* – epta chiliades
Επτά χιλιάδες

8000 – *Eight Thousand* – okto chiliades
Οκτώ χιλιάδες

9000 – *Nine Thousand* – ennia chiliades
Εννιά χιλιάδες

10,000 – *Ten Thousand* – deka chiliades
Δέκα χιλιάδες

20,000 – *Twenty Thousand* – eikosi chiliades
Είκοσι χιλιάδες

30,000 – *Thirty Thousand* – trianta chiliades
Τριάντα χιλιάδες

40,000 – *Forty Thousand* – saranta chiliades
Σαράντα χιλιάδες

50,000 – *Fifty Thousand* – peninta chiliades
Πενήντα χιλιάδες

100,000 – *One Hundred Thousand* – ekato chiliades
Εκατό χιλιάδες

200,000 – *Two hundred Thousand* – diakosies chiliades
Διακόσιες χιλιάδες

300,000 - *Three Hundred Thousand* – triakosies chiliades
   Τριακόσιες χιλιάδες

1,000,000 – *One Million* – ena ekatomirio
   Ένα εκατομμύριο

2,000,000 – *Two Million* – dio ekatomiria
   Δύο εκατομμύρια

3,000,000 – *Three Million* – tria ekatomiria
   Τρία εκατομμύρια

10,000,000 – *Ten Million* – deka ekatomiria
   Δέκα εκατομμύρια

100,000,000 – *One Hundred Million* – ekato ekatomiria
   Εκατό εκατομμύρια

1,000,000,000 – *One Billion* – ena disekatomirio
   Ένα δισεκατομμύριο

Example: 5,678,901 – *Five Million Six Hundred Seventy Eight Thousand Nine Hundred Paradigma: One* – pente ekatomiria exakosia evdominta okto chiliades enniakosia ena
   Παράδειγμα: Πέντε εκατομμύρια εξακόσια εβδομήντα οκτώ χιλιάδες εννιακόσια ένα

PART XXXVII

ORDINAL NUMBERS

► **Click Here for the .mp3 Audio**

1st – *First* – protos
Πρώτος

2nd – *Second* – defteros
Δεύτερος

3rd – *Third* – tritos
Τρίτος

4th – *Fourth* – tetartos
Τέταρτος

5th – *Fifth* – pemptos

πέμπτος

6th – *Sixth* – ektos
έκτος

7th – *Seventh* – evdomos
Έβδομος

8th – *Eighth* – ogdoos
όγδοος

9th – *Ninth* – enatos
ένατος

10th – *Tenth* – dekatos
Δέκατος

11th – *Eleventh* – endekatos
Ενδέκατος

12th – *Twelfth* – dodekatos
Δωδέκατος

13th – *Thirteenth* – dekatos tritos
Δέκατος τρίτος

14th – *Fourteenth* – dekatos tetartos
Δέκατος τέταρτος

144

15**th** – *Fifteenth* – dekatos pemptos
Δέκατος πέμπτος

16**th** – *Sixteenth* – dekatos ektos
Δέκατος έκτος

17**th** – *Seventeenth* – dekatos evdomos
Δέκατος έβδομος

18**th** – *Eighteenth* – dekatos ogdoos
Δέκατος όγδοος

19**th** – *Nineteenth* – dekatos enatos
Δέκατος ένατος

20**th** – *Twentieth* – ikostos
εικοστός

PART XXXVIII

TIME

► **Click Here for the .mp3 Audio**

Minutes – lepta
   Λεπτά

Hours – ores
   Ώρες

12:00 – *Twelve O'clock* – dodeka i ora
   Δώδεκα η ώρα

1:00 – *One O'clock* – mia i ora
   Μία η ώρα

2:00 – *Two O'clock* – dio i ora
   Δύο η ώρα

3:00 – *Three O'clock* – tris i ora
　　Τρεις η ώρα

4:00 – *Four O'clock* – tesseris i ora
　　Τέσσερις η ώρα

5:00 – *Five O'clock* – pente i ora
　　Πέντε η ώρα

6:00 – *Six O'clock* – exi i ora
　　Έξι η ώρα

7:00 – *Seven O'clock* – epta i ora
　　Επτά η ώρα

8:00 – *Eight O'clock* – okto i ora
　　Οκτώ η ώρα

9:00 – *Nine O'clock* – ennea i ora
　　Εννέα η ώρα

10:00 – *Ten O'clock* – deka i ora
　　Δέκα η ώρα

11:00 – *Eleven O'clock* – enteka i ora
　　Έντεκα η ώρα

2:30 – *Two and a half* – dio kai misi
　　Δύο και μισή

3:30 – *Three and a half* – tris kai misi
  Τρεις και μισή

4:30 – *Four Thirty* – tesseris kai misi
  Τέσσερις και μισή

5:15 – *Five Fifteen* – pente kai tetarto
  Πέντε και τέταρτο

6:15 – *Six Fifteen* – exi kai tetarto
  Έξι και τέταρτο

6:45 – *Six Fourty Five* – epta para tetarto
  Επτά παρά τέταρο

7:45 – *Quarter until Eight* – okto para tetarto
  Οκτώ παρά τέταρτο

7:50 – *Ten Until Eight* – okto para deka
  Οκτώ παρά δέκα

12:00am – 11:59am – *In the morning* – dodeka ta charamata me dodeka pro mesimvrias – to proi
  Δώδεκα τα χαράματα με δώδεκα προ μεσημβρίας (πμ) – το πρωί

12:00pm – 5:59pm – *In the afternoon* – dodeka meta mesimvrias me exi meta mesimvrias – to apogevma
  Δώδεκα μετά μεσημβρίας (μμ) με έξι μετά μεσημβρίας (μμ) – το απόγευμα

6:00pm – 11:59pm – *In the night* – exi meta mesimvrias me dodeka to vradi – ti nichta
Έξι μετά μεσημβρίας (μμ) με δώδεκα το βράδυ – τη νύχτα

12:00pm – *Mid Day* – mesimeri
12:00 μμ – μεσημέρι

12:00am – *Mid Night* – mesanichta
12:00 πμ – μεσάνυχτα

What time is it? – ti ora ine?
Τι ώρα είναι

It is (time) – ine (ora)
Είναι (ώρα)

In how many minutes? – se posa lepta?
Σε πόσα λεπτά

In how many hours? – Se poses ores?
Σε πόσες ώρες

What time do we arrive? – Ti ora ftanoume?
Τι ώρα φτάνουμε

What time do we leave? – Ti ora fevgoume?
Τι ώρα φεύγουμε

It's late – Ine arga
Είναι αργά

It's early – Ine noris
  Είναι νωρίς

Later – argotera
  Αργότερα

I'm sorry I am late – Signomi pou argisa
  Συγγνώμη που άργησα

PART XXXIX

DAYS & MONTHS

► **Click Here for the .mp3 Audio**

Day – imera
   Ημέρα

Week – evdomada
   Εβδομάδα

Month – minas
   Μήνας

Monday – Deftera
   Δευτέρα

Tuesday – Triti
   Τρίτη

Wednesday – Tetarti
Τετάρτη

Thursday – Pempti
Πέμπτη

Friday – paraskevi
Παρασκευή

Saturday – Savato
Σάββατο

Sunday – Kiriaki
Κυριακή

What day of the week is it? – Ti mera ine?
Τι μέρα είναι

Today is (day) – Simera ine (imera)
Σήμερα είναι (ημέρα)

First Week – proti evdomada
Πρώτη εβδομάδα

Second Week – defter evdomada
Δεύτερη εβδομάδα

January – Ianouarios
Ιανουάριος

February – Fevrouarios
  Φεβρουάριος

March – Martios
  Μάρτιος

April – Aprilios
  Απρίλιος

May – Maios
  Μάϊος

June – Iounios
  Ιούνιος

July – Ioulios
  Ιούλιος

August – Avgoustos
  Αύγουστος

September – Septemvrios
  Σεπτέμβριος

October – Oktovrios
  Οκτώβριος

November – Noemvrios
  Νοέμβριος

December – Dekemvrios
Δεκέμβριος

PART XL

COLORS

► **Click Here for the .mp3 Audio**

What colors do you have? – Ti chromata echis?
Τι χρώματα έχεις

Do you have a different color? – Echis allo chroma?
Έχεις άλλο χρώμα

What is your favorite color? – Pio ine to agapimeno sou chroma?
Ποιο είναι το αγαπημένο σου χρώμα

My favorite color is (color) – To agapimeno mou chroma ine (chroma)
Το αγαπημένο μου χρώμα είναι (χρώμα)

Black – mavro

155

Μαύρο

White – aspro/lefko
Άσπρο/Λευκό

Red – kokkino
Κόκκινο

Blue – ble
Μπλε

Green – Prasino
Πράσινο

Yellow – kitrino
Κίτρινο

Orange – Portokali
Πορτοκαλί

Brown – kafe
Καφέ

Gray – gkri
Γκρι

Pink – roz
Ροζ

Purple – mov
Μωβ

PART XLI

WEATHER

► **Click Here for the .mp3 Audio**

What is the weather like? – Ti kero kani?
    Τι καιρό κάνει

What is the temperature? – Ti thermokrasia echi?
    Τι θερμοκρασία έχει

What is the weather forecast? – Ti ipe to deltio kerou?
    Τι είπε το δελτίο καιρού

It is (number) degrees – Echi (arithmos) vathmous
    Έχει (αριθμός) βαθμούς

It is sunny – Echi ilio
    Έχει ήλιο

It is raining– Vrechi
    Βρέχει

It is going to rain – Tha vrexi
    Θα βρέξει

It is hot – Echi zesti
    Έχει ζέστη

It is cold – Echi krio
    Έχει κρύο
    It is windy – Fisai
    Φυσάει

It is snowing – Chionizi
    Χιονίζει

It is freezing – Kani pagonia
    Κάνει παγωνιά

It is cloudy – Echi sinefia
    Έχει συνεφιά

What terrible weather we're having – Ti apesio kero pou echoume
    Τι απαίσιο καιρό που έχουμε

What nice weather we're having – Ti oreo kero pou echoume
    Τι ωραίο καιρό που έχουμε

Made in United States
North Haven, CT
04 May 2024

52085749R00096